IN THE EYE OF THE CATHOLIC STORM

THE CHURCH SINCE VATICAN II

IN THE EYE OF THE CATHOLIC STORM
THE CHURCH SINCE VATICAN II

**MARY JO LEDDY
BISHOP REMI DE ROO
& DOUGLAS ROCHE**

EDITED AND WITH AN INTRODUCTION BY MICHAEL CREAL

HarperPerennial
HarperCollins*Publishers*Ltd

First Edition

Canadian Cataloguing in Publication Data

Leddy, Mary Joanna, 1946-
    In the eye of the Catholic storm

ISBN 0-00-637757-2

1. Church and social problems — Catholic Church. I. De Roo, Remi J.
2. Roche, Douglas, 1929- . III. Creal, Michael.

HN37.C3L4 1992   261.8   C92-093026-3

92 93 94 95 96 AG 5 4 3 2 1

CONTENTS

A BRIEF CHRONOLOGY

1869-70   First Vatican Council

1891   *Rerum Novarum*: Leo XIII's encyclical on
            social and economic issues

1958   Election of John XXIII

1959   John XXIII announces that a Vatican
            Council will be convened

1962 (Oct.) Opening session of Vatican II

1963   Death of John XXIII; election of Paul VI

1965 (Dec.) Closing session of Vatican II

1968   Conference of Latin American bishops at
            Medellín

DOCUMENTS CITED

Vatican II Documents

1964 *Unitatis Redintegratio* — Decree on Ecumenism

1964 *Lumen Gentium* — Dogmatic Constitution on the Church

1964 *Orientalium Ecclesiarum* — Decree on the Eastern Churches

1965 *Perfectae Caritatis* — Decree on the Renewal of Religious Life

1965 *Nostra Aetate* — Declaration on the Relation of the Church to Non-Christian Religions

1965 *Dignitatis Humanae* — Declaration on Religious Liberty

1965 *Presbyterorum Ordinis* — Decree on Priests

1965 *Gaudium et Spes* — Pastoral Constitution on the Church in the Modern World (often referred to as "The Church in the Modern World")

Other Magisterial Texts

1963 *Pacem in Terris* (John XXIII) — Encyclical on Peace

1967 *Populorum Progressio* (Paul VI) — Encyclical on Development

1968 *Humanae Vitae* (Paul VI) — Encyclical on Regulation of Births

1968 Statement of Canadian Bishops on *Humanae Vitae*

1971 *Convenientes ex Universo* — Synod of Bishops Statement on Justice in the World

1981 *Laborem Exercens* (John Paul II) — Encyclical on Work

1983 "Ethical Reflections on the Economic Crisis" — Statement of the Canadian Conference of Catholic Bishops

IN THE EYE OF THE CATHOLIC STORM

THE CHURCH SINCE VATICAN II

INTRODUCTION

The setting for the series of conversations which constitutes this book was the Pastoral Centre of the Diocese of Victoria on Vancouver Island. For a week in January 1991, the very heavens conspired to keep the three participants in concentrated dialogue, as one of the worst storms in recent decades buried Victoria under a couple of feet of snow. It was practically impossible to venture out even for a walk during the first three days so, almost without interruption, mornings, afternoons and evenings were spent working through the various issues that make up the chapters of this book. The book was created, one could say, in the eye of the storm.

At the end of each afternoon session we would celebrate the Eucharist around Bishop De Roo's dining-room table. There was a time of relaxation before dinner, but because war in the Middle East seemed imminent that week, "free time" conversation was largely focused on the Gulf Crisis. Still, it was a warm atmosphere and there was lots of laughter during and between the work sessions.

In a symbolic sense, the weather provided exactly the right setting for these discussions, because they focused on questions which are creating no small amount of turbulence in the Catholic Church today. Indeed, the whole book is written in what might be called the eye of the Catholic storm.

How did the book come to be?

In 1968, Remi J. De Roo, the Bishop of Victoria, and Douglas Roche, a prominent Catholic layman and journalist, wrote a book that reflected the new spirit of openness generated by the Second Vatican Council. Entitled *Man to Man,** it was a frank conversation about the revolutionary implications of Vatican II. That such an honest exchange had become possible between a bishop and a layman spoke volumes about the impact of that momentous gathering convened by Pope John XXIII in 1962. The first Vatican Council had assembled almost a century earlier and had asserted the Church's authority in opposition to modernity and all its "errors." Vatican II, on the other hand, sought to open up the Church to all that was valuable in the modern world and to rethink its mission in that spirit. The Church came to be seen in a new light — as the "People of God" — and the laity were no longer to be relegated to a passive role, accepting without question whatever was given them from above. The conversation between Douglas Roche and Remi De Roo reflected that new understanding and ranged over the great issues that had emerged during the Council: how decisions were to be made, how all Christians were equal in baptism, how the Church's role was to serve the world and not dominate it, how change was required in relations with other Christian bodies and other world religions. These — and other such important matters — made up the agenda of that book, which reflected much of the Second Vatican Council's excitement and hope.

Some changes wrought by Vatican II — in liturgical practice, for instance — were clearly irreversible. In other areas it

* Milwaukee Bruce Publishing, 1969, Gary MacEoin, editor.

seemed, as the years went by, that the hope and promise of the Council would not be fulfilled. The new freedom, and the speed of changes occurring in the Church, frightened those who feared an unraveling of the whole Catholic tradition. A conservative reaction began to set in. In the same period, new movements in the Latin American Church and in other parts of the Third World signaled a stirring of the Spirit that opened up possibilities (and problems) far beyond anything imagined at Vatican II. The impetus for some of these new movements — like Bible study in "base communities" — had certainly come from the Council. But because base communities (of which there are tens of thousands in Latin America) were communities of lay people who came together to worship, read the Bible and discuss the personal and social implications of the Bible for their own lives, there was often a radical political edge to such groups, and this led them into conflict with political authorities and sometimes with ecclesiastical authorities. And the "preferential option for the poor" taken by the Latin American bishops at their meeting in Puebla, Mexico, in 1979 may have had its theological roots in conciliar decrees, but there is no doubt that it called for a radical new focus on the causes as well as the effects of poverty, and raised further concerns in conservative circles. Traditional ways of formulating social teaching were being challenged and traditional patterns of authority appeared to be in question.

During the same period, in the decades following the Council, the world as a whole underwent vast changes. Economic conditions in the Third World grew more desperate. The wealthiest nation in the world became the world's most indebted nation. The Cold War appeared to have ended but the early optimism was dispelled by the dangers of political and economic disorder in the Soviet Union and continuing violence in the Middle East (among other places). And in affluent parts of the world, the obsession with consumer goods on the one hand, and the relentless competitive struggle on the other (which, not so incidentally, left great numbers of people on the margin of society), were not exactly marks of social well-being. In fact, a whole new body of literature was beginning to emerge that described a spiritual vacuum in North American and Western society.

It seemed the right moment to try once again to "discern the signs of the times," to use a New Testament phrase which assumed great prominence at the Vatican Council. It seemed a good moment to reassess Vatican II, to ask what had happened to its vision, to ask where in the world the Church was in the 1990s.

But if there was to be another serious dialogue on such questions, it certainly couldn't be "man to man"! One of the momentous changes in the past couple of decades has been a recognition on the part of many people — women first, but also increasing numbers of men — that women's voices have generally gone unheeded in our culture and within the Church. A discussion about the Church and the world that did not include a woman's voice would be unthinkable today.

So when Remi De Roo and Douglas Roche discussed the idea of reassessing the vision of Vatican II, considering where things stood in the Church of the nineties and exploring new possibilities for the future, they invited one of the most articulate Catholic women in North America to join their dialogue. It was an inspired idea; not only was Mary Jo Leddy's perspective fresh and distinctive, but her presence introduced a new dynamic. Her ideas, which were often profound and challenging, opened up new social and theological dimensions.

The whole week was a very powerful experience for me. I had been invited to be a kind of facilitator, and to edit the transcripts of the dozen or so sessions. The fact that I was an Anglican, teaching Humanities and Religious Studies at York University, could have made me feel a bit of an outsider, but

such was not the case. It was not just that these three remark-
ably gifted people — and admirable human beings — became
my friends during that week, though I am deeply grateful for
that. It was also that the quality of the dialogue matched — at
the very least — anything I have ever experienced. Though
they are all Catholics, these three came from very different
places and are very different people. Remi De Roo has been
in the priesthood all his adult life and has been a bishop for
almost thirty years. Douglas Roche has been a journalist,
Member of Parliament, Canadian Ambassador for Disarmament at the United Nations, academic, husband and father.
Mary Jo Leddy was a senior in high school when the Vatican
Council was convened, so in the early sixties she was busy
playing basketball and going to dances. When she finished
her secondary education, she joined a religious order which,
within months, was undergoing vast changes as a direct result
of Vatican II.

Each was indelibly marked by the Council. Remi De Roo
became a bishop at the time Vatican II was convened, so his
episcopal ministry began in the context of that new vision and
has been lived out in its light. Doug Roche covered the event
as a journalist and underwent a kind of personal transformation as a result of his experience. For Mary Jo Leddy, the
Council was the context within which she began her life as a
religious. It has been a given in her adult life.

When I arrived in Victoria, I wondered if there would be
too much in common among these three, but I quickly learned
that their different backgrounds guaranteed three quite distinctive voices. (The opposite possibility, of course, was a fundamental breakdown in communication, because a conversation
between three people from such different situations could
have been a standoff.) What I began to sense, as we worked
our way into the important and difficult questions which constituted the agenda for that week, was that this was perhaps a

microcosm of the Church as it had been envisioned at Vatican
II. Here were three Christians, each engaged in a distinctive
ministry, listening to each other with enormous respect, hearing things that came out of different areas of experience. But
in the overall conversation, it was clear that no one of them
had the final word, and none claimed to. Here was the sort of
mutuality and quality of dialogue that could really build community. If this was an example of "church," then "church"
meant being honest, open, self-critical, caring, searching,
hopeful and faithful to the promise of the Gospel. The importance of these qualities is beyond dispute at an intellectual or
theological level, but in real life there are formidable barriers
which tend to separate clergy and laity, bishops and clergy, and
men and women, when fundamental policies and practices are
at stake. Those barriers were simply not in evidence during
that week in Victoria.

This is not to say that you as a reader will not detect real
differences in this dialogue, differences of viewpoint which
are worth careful examination. Douglas Roche's involvement
in questions of peace and disarmament and Third World
development lead him to insist that the Church address certain issues without delay; that the Church's voice be heard
loudly and clearly as offering moral leadership where questions of fundamental justice or the future of the planet are
hanging in the balance. Remi De Roo's social, theological and
pastoral perspectives give him a breadth of understanding, a
patience and a hopefulness that are impressive in their depth.
The distinctiveness and originality of Mary Jo Leddy's views
of both contemporary society and culture on the one hand,
and the meaning of Christian vocation on the other, make her
voice one that speaks to Christians of many traditions, as well
as to thoughtful people whose experience is entirely secular.

As all three participants in the dialogue would readily
agree, this book does not settle all the complex and ambiguous

problems of our time. When people struggle with such questions in genuine dialogue, they don't achieve perfect clarity on every issue. But in my view this book addresses those matters in a way that offers a pattern for continuing Christian inquiry and debate. Conversation in this spirit would breathe life into every part of the contemporary Church — and the contemporary world.

Note: In the final editing stages of the book, it was agreed that some reflections on the Gulf War might be added to the chapter on "War and Peace." In early May of 1991, a conference call was arranged between Remi De Roo in Victoria, Douglas Roche in Edmonton and Mary Jo Leddy and the editor in Toronto. There was no thought that this would be a definitive assessment of the Gulf War, but it seemed highly appropriate for each of the three participants to reflect on the particular implications of that war in the light of their discussion of the larger questions of war and peace. It would have been inappropriate to try to integrate this material into the text of the earlier dialogue, so it has been added as a "postscript" to the chapter.

Michael Creal

✠ I ✠

VATICAN II:
FADING DREAM OR
ENDURING HOPE?

Roche: Pope John XXIII convened the Second Vatican Council to allow the Church to respond creatively to the issues and challenges of the modern world. The Council has been described as opening up the windows and letting fresh air into the Church. But of course it was more than that — it was a rediscovery of what the Church really is. The affirmation of the equality of all Christians in baptism gave profound new dimensions to our understanding of the Church. To recognize our equality was a major break with the past. The old triumphalism of the hierarchial Church was to be replaced with a more open and listening response to the world around it. The great documents of the Council concerning the Church's role in the modern world redefined the Church's presence in the social order, in a secular world, in a world of other religious traditions. It was a new venturing out and it began with great hope.

Leddy: What were you doing at the time, Doug?

Roche: I was a journalist for the U.S. Catholic magazine *Sign*, and I spent considerable time at Vatican II writing about it.

De Roo: What were your feelings about the Council? What did it mean to you personally?

Roche: Vatican II liberated me as a Catholic. I had grown up very much in the enclosure of the Catholic Church, with its reliance on piety and devotions, and with special reverence, on a sort of pedestal level, for the priest, let alone the bishop, who was a faraway figure.

Let me tell you what I think were the principal gains of Vatican II. These certainly affected me personally as they affected the whole Church.

The first was the affirmation of the Church as the People of God. For me, this was a new, radical definition. It meant the Church was no longer to be thought of as a vertical structure, beginning with the Pope and the bishops, followed by the clergy and then perhaps the sisters, and finally with the laity on the bottom. Vatican II made it clear that baptism gave us equality. My point is demonstrated rather dramatically by the insertion of the chapter on the "People of God" *before* the chapter on the hierarchy in the basic Constitution on the Church, *Lumen Gentium.*

The second was the Eucharist, and the understanding that the unity of the Church was both expressed and brought about by the Eucharist. And the reason this was such a major change was that it placed the Eucharist rather than the papacy at the center of Christian unity.

The third was the emphasis on scripture; that opened up real communication with Protestants. It made the ecumenical advances of Vatican II possible.

Next was the concept of pluralism, which replaced the singleness of view which had prevailed in the Catholic Church. Theological pluralism was manifest at Vatican II because the Council brought back in to the center of discussion some of those very figures who previously had been banned by the Church, like Henri de Lubac and Teilhard de Chardin. The respect for genuine diversity that came out of Vatican II was extremely important. The different theological interpretations were seen to be not conflicting but complementary. And out of that came a hierarchy of truths which enable us to establish correct priorities. Consider a minor example. I myself think that eating fish on Friday is not such a bad idea. It's a small penance in life. But to equate eating meat on Friday with grosser forms of misconduct, as we did in the pre-conciliar Church, is pretty silly. The ecumenical dimension, theological dialogue, praying together with other Christians, cooperation between churches, all that had been forbidden in the pre-conciliar Church.

Finally, but not last in importance, were the justice and peace issues. The major cultural, economic, political and military problems of the modern world were tackled head on in the Council debates and in the documents that grew out of them. All this was very exciting and very important.

Those were the things at Vatican II that really affected me.

Leddy: What were you doing, Remi, when the Council began?

De Roo: At the end of October 1962, I was not only informed that I was called to be Bishop of Victoria, I was also called to the Council. So before my ordination, which occurred later (on December 14), I flew to Rome and spent two weeks there. I was really thrilled at the enthusiasm I picked up and the sense of history in the making. Over three thousand bishops and theologians — it was the largest-ever official

Catholic leadership assembly in the history of the Church. And that awesome atmosphere in St. Peter's in my first experience as a bishop-elect certainly marked me for life. Before the Council ended in 1965, I had four opportunities to address the Assembly, and the opportunity to submit papers on a number of subjects.

Leddy: Just out of curiosity, what did you speak on, Remi?

De Roo: The unique world of the laity and their ministry. The sacramental sanctity of marriage — that speech got transmitted around the world in several languages, because I had consulted married people on Vancouver Island, and that made news, that this bishop had consulted his people before speaking. An intervention on priesthood. I also submitted a proposal about hermits. The hermetic discipline, lost for centuries in the Western Church, was restored on Vancouver Island — I don't know if you were aware of that. Most important of all, I made a speech about the unity of God's creative and redemptive plan. That was in consultation with key figures like Congar, Chenu and Tillard.

But I have another vivid memory. The Canadian bishops had an audience with Pope John XXIII and I was introduced to him by Cardinal Léger. Pope John later presented me with the personal gift of a ring, calling me the Benjamin of the Canadian bishops. When I arrived in Victoria and stated that I was coming to live the Vatican Council with the people of Vancouver Island, they gave me a very warm response.

Leddy: I'm probably about twenty years younger than the two of you, and I've been trying to think back on my experience of Vatican II. At that time I was a senior in high school, going to football games and dances, and I really didn't know what was going on. The teachers were talking about an Ecumenical

Council but it was truly Greek to me. I had absolutely no sense of its significance. I was just your average Catholic kid, a committed Catholic but not a conscious, reflecting Catholic at that point in my life. I've thought about this a lot because it's probably indicative of a whole generational experience.

My own experience of the traditional Church was quite positive, in that I grew up in a small, believing community on the prairies. It was not an institutional church, really. It was a community. Everybody knew everybody. There was no heavy-duty clericalism. No heavy-duty episcopal interference. It was a church sustained by symbols and a real sense of community.

Well, Vatican II was still in process when I joined a religious congregation, and I joined the traditional model. As far as I knew, it was always going to be that way. I remember quite distinctly when we received the habit and were told that we would be buried in this habit, that this was a commitment for life. Six months later we were out of the habit, and that taught me the ephemeral quality of much of what we think is absolute.

But I guess the point I want to make is that I didn't feel the need for Vatican II. It happened but it wasn't something I'd been longing for. I didn't feel any deep need for change. So when Vatican II came to my little corner of the world, it was more the natural evolution of a relatively communal sense of the Church. The greater openness it promised already existed on the prairies.

But back to the religious congregation I joined. We talked a lot about the Vatican Decree on the Renewal of Religious Life (*Perfectae Caritatis*), and in spite of the fact that the Vatican has tried to exercise some control over religious orders, the wonderful insight of that document remains. It said that religious life is a charismatic dimension of the Church. The key words were that it is a "gift to the Church," a gift of the

Spirit *to* the Church. It was not a gift *from* the Church nor was it something to be "controlled" by the Church.

De Roo: I want to pick up on that point about a gift of the Spirit, in terms of renewal. The vision that gradually emerged from the Council was that of a renewed humanity in which the Church would play a reconciling role expressing the love of Christ to the world, with faith in the ongoing presence of the Spirit working through many different forms of human experience. Another way to put it is to say that, for the first time in history, we saw the possibility of Catholicity combining with democracy. After all, the Church is historical. It has identified with many forms of human experience throughout the centuries. The particular awakening of human consciousness that we call democracy was something to be welcomed. As Doug has pointed out, the gifts of the Spirit in baptism are given to all, and from them flow mutuality, collegiality, personal responsibility, extending to the responsibility of every local church, every religious community.

Leddy: As I understand it, the central and unifying vision of Vatican II was that God is present in the whole of creation and that religion is not confined to a particular place or a particular people or a particular way of doing things. This vision was a faith vision; it wasn't just about the world, it was about God. It was a sense of who God is and how God is.

But I have to go back to another part of my experience of those years of the Council. In some ways, it was a period of enormous upheaval. Many sisters left their communities. What struck me, as a younger person, was that the traditional model must have been quite empty because so many people left with such ease. The model had grown empty and some profound change was needed — not just changes but *change*.

I think it was only when I started to do my graduate studies on the Holocaust that I really began to understand what Vatican II was all about. I saw how the silence of the Church at the time of the Holocaust meant that people had died, people had been killed because there wasn't a visible or vocal ethical resistance. I began to understand what had been wrong with the Church and what the people at Vatican II had been trying to say and do. The Vatican Decree on Ecumenism was a momentous thing. It wasn't *everything*, but in terms of the long span of Church history it was something.

All that might have remained just an intellectual realization for me except for the fact that, in 1976, a group of us in Toronto started a newspaper, the *Catholic New Times*. We started it because we began to feel the chill, the conservative chill, in the Church. And that's when I began to struggle for Vatican II. Before that I had taken it for granted. For me, it was just the way things were, just the way the Church was. Then we began to see that many people weren't taking it for granted. It was through the newspaper that I came into contact not with the "traditional" Church but with the institutional, bureaucratic power structure that was defending itself mightily against change. I was shocked at the coercive power trips that were going on, all in the name of defending "the Church."

Roche: This is the kind of thing that concerns me, the closing down of the debate that began with Vatican II. The openness that was present then is missing today. There is growing evidence of resistance to the change that was mandated by John XXIII. How many bishops have been appointed in the last ten years who really want to keep alive and extend the spirit of Vatican II? Each of us has referred to the excitement and promise of the Council, but now I think we have to recognize that the current trend is in the opposite direction. I don't think what Vatican II said can be snuffed out, I don't think it can be reversed at its core, but it is definitely jeopardized today by the intransigent attitude of those in charge of the Church, who have slowed down and impeded the cause of reform. As I said, the trend is against Vatican II, and I think we should focus on that trend.

Leddy: I think what we've seen in the years since Vatican II is that many of its ideals and principles and insights were never built into the institution. In fact, the institutional dimension of the Church is now jeopardizing them. The principle that I see most in jeopardy at the moment is what was called at Vatican II — correct me if I'm wrong — the principle of "subsidiarity." What this meant was that the authority to make decisions would be given to the appropriate sphere of responsibility, and that that authority would not be taken over by any other authority. I think that was a very important principle. It was saying that not all authority resides in Rome, that there is an authority appropriate to bishops, to religious congregations, to national churches and to local churches, and that those authorities cannot be overridden. Now I see that principle to be very much in jeopardy. In fact, the Vatican — I'm not saying the Pope here — has taken unto itself decisions that belong to other levels of authority. That has been the cause of a great deal of difficulty. And the national churches need to make pastoral decisions appropriate to their context, and that too is in jeopardy, and so we have a whole series of questions around ministry. What is the role of the priest? What Church structures and what forms of ministry are appropriate in different situations? These issues are incapable of resolution as long as there has to be one solution for the whole Church throughout the entire world. While Vatican II talked about unity, it is now being interpreted as uniformity.

It seems to me — and few will dispute this point, I think — that women religious in the Americas were the group that most immediately and completely took up the challenge of Vatican II. We took it up, we ran with it, we struggled and we changed. We changed our structures, our way of life, we changed everything to be in harmony with the ideals of Vatican II. And it wasn't easy, because we had to struggle with the whole weight of our own traditions. But we did it. We didn't have any part in shaping Vatican II — I mean our voice was not there — but we took it up and we lived it, with a fullness and commitment that perhaps no other group in the Church did. We have really lived with its promise and we have lived with the struggle of achieving that promise. And what follows from that is that probably no other group has experienced to the same extent the Church's reaction against Vatican II. We have felt the heavy hand of the Vatican in a way that few others have. And not just recently. I'm talking about over a ten-year period. And you know, there are only so many options you have when you're faced with this. You can get out of the institutional Church or you can capitulate or you can try to find some kind of peace in the midst of it.

But aside from all this, Vatican II is in trouble because it wasn't complete enough. There were too many voices left out of it. Like women. Like the poor. I also think that Vatican II is threatened because all of us underestimated the fact that what it called for was really a change of heart, a profound conversion. It isn't enough just to have new theologies. It isn't enough just to have new structural forms, or institutional change. There remains for each one of us — and for all of us together — a call to a profound conversion.

De Roo: I'm very happy, Mary Jo, that you touched on the question of the poor as one of the limitations of Vatican II; it was certainly not complete in this respect. This is a point we must come back to later. We must also return to the question of the place of women. But I want to add three points which I think are complementary to what you have just said. They refer to major new doctrinal insights of Vatican II that today remain at risk.

The first one relates to the document on religious freedom, *Dignitatis Humanae*. Religious freedom is the right of the *person* as distinct from the right of truth. That document reversed the traditional stance that "error has no rights." That common view was very influential and had significant consequences in the discipline and teaching of the Church before Vatican II. It justified the Church's use of coercion where people were "in error." *Dignitatis Humanae* points to the sacredness of the human person. It affirms the autonomy of conscience properly informed, and respects dissent in matters that are not authoritatively defined as integral to revelation. This teaching was affirmed at Vatican II but today stands at risk.

Secondly, in the documents on unity or ecumenism, *Unitatis Redintegratio*, and on Eastern churches, *Orientalium Ecclesiarum*, Vatican II solemnly declared the right of the churches of the East to rule themselves. Here is a theological principle which affirms collegiality and diversity not only in matters of discipline but also in the recognition of cultural diversity, which amounts to a certain pluralism in teaching. We admitted in the decree on unity that this principle had not always been honored in the past — there was an admission of guilt in this area on the part of the Church. We are experiencing serious difficulties on this point today. We seem to be regressing to older patterns. As you said, Mary Jo, unity tends to be understood as uniformity.

And thirdly, in the "Decree on Priests" (*Presbyterorum Ordinis*), Article 16, for the first time in history we linked priesthood and marriage by recognizing and commending the

Eastern married clergy. We said there, in an indirect way, that sexuality is not to be understood as a lesser good (let alone a weakness) but that it can be joined with priesthood and be complementary to it. And that opens up a major question that we have not yet come to grips with. If it is theologically and pastorally appropriate to have married clergy in the Eastern churches, and if it is accepted in the West under certain circumstances, a serious problem of inconsistency arises. It's not just a logical inconsistency; it's more serious than that. It has significant practical, pastoral implications. We have affirmed the right of the people to have the Eucharist but sometimes there are not enough priests available to make that right a reality. A mandatory celibate priesthood doesn't help. This is a subject that causes friction and conflict. Ultimately it calls for resolution one way or another. Today, however, serious reconsideration is resisted.

Roche: Conflict and friction. I think Remi De Roo has pinpointed three important areas where fidelity to Vatican II is at risk. And let's face it — this is not simply a matter of abstract analysis. There is a crisis. I appreciated, Mary Jo, what you said about the sisters "living" Vatican II and yet feeling the heavy hand of the Vatican as a result. And I must say that I do not take lightly the statement issued by the Catholic Theological Society of America in the United States and Canada, on the twenty-fifth anniversary of the close of Vatican II, entitled "Do Not Extinguish the Spirit." This major statement, which identifies the achievements of Vatican II, calls our attention to the need for *continued* renewal if the Spirit is not to be extinguished in the North American Church (and, by extension, the Church everywhere). The theologians are emphasizing that the very collegiality of the bishops that was a hallmark of Vatican II has been diminished. The role of episcopal conferences has been downgraded by the Vatican.

The manner in which bishops are chosen does not conform with the conciliar emphasis on the right of local churches to govern themselves; a local diocese has little say in the selection of its bishop. The theologians who prepared that statement emphasize that cutting off theologians (and we all know of eminent ones who have been cut off by the misuse of Vatican authority) has shut down that very theological expression which the Council engendered in the first place. The theologians who issued the statement view feminism as a sign of the times and call our attention to the diminishment of women by the authorities, not only by ruling them out as candidates for the priesthood but also by submerging their input.

And it's not only the theologians who are speaking. Some forty-five hundred Catholics in the United States signed a statement at the twenty-fifth anniversary of Vatican II entitled "A Call for Reform in the Catholic Church." It's a poignant call for the Church to deal in a more vigorous manner with the problems which today are fracturing humanity: poverty, drugs, environmental destruction and the excesses of militarism. It calls our attention to the declining pastoral service in the Church resulting from the crisis of the priesthood, which is caused in significant measure by the persistent, authoritarian refusal of the Church at official levels even to examine the question of celibacy. And all of this is connected to the fact that the laity, sisters, priests are denied access to the decision-making processes of the Church. When synods of bishops are still maintained in secrecy, it does not inspire confidence among the laity that the "People of God" are understood today as they were in conciliar thinking. In my view, all these things jeopardize the processes and achievements of Vatican II.

On the other hand, it's clear that while Vatican II is under attack in many quarters, its spirit remains very much alive. It's not just that we have to get *back* to Vatican II — we have to go beyond it. And to do that we have to identify and address the critical questions in today's world. To identify some of the deepest questions requires a kind of prophetic gift. Other questions are more obvious: the question of poverty in the face of luxury; the danger of war when military technology threatens total destruction; the nature of human sexuality; the oppression of women; the meaning of spirituality. The whole world faces these questions. And if we follow Vatican II at its deepest level, these questions are our proper agenda today.

✠ II ✠

PROPHETS AT RISK

De Roo: As I study the Scriptures, it seems to me that prophets always arose when they were needed. Prophecy has to do with reading the signs of the times; Vatican II reminded us of that. But reading the signs of the times requires a certain spiritual alertness. Part of our problem is that we have been lulled to sleep by the soporific effect of a number of modern myths. For instance, the myth of progress, which sees evolution as linear, historical and automatic. There is also the myth that reason alone can solve all human problems. As we come to think that we can reason our way out of every impasse, we are led to believe that there is really no need for prophecy.

I believe we must broaden our understanding of prophecy and rediscover the prophecy of the heart. I have in mind the Vaniers, the Martin Luther Kings, the Mother Theresas and others who may not speak much but who offer prophecy in powerful symbolic gestures. And that kind of prophecy is also found in critical historical events. I think it was found in Vatican II.

Prophecy is a gift to the Church and it belongs to the Church as a whole, so I never trust an individual who claims to be a prophet. We have to remember that prophets are rarely recognized when they are alive. The self-proclaimed turn out not to be prophets at all. Only historical discernment can finally distinguish the true from the false. That's a big issue of the Old Testament: there was constant struggle about who were the real and who were the pseudo-prophets; about who really discerned the signs of the times.

One of the things about Vatican II that really excited me was that the Council put everything in the perspective of the Reign of God rather than focusing too much on the Church itself. For that reason, it opened the way for a new era of prophecy. Walter Brueggemann's book *The Prophetic Imagination** traces the story of prophecy. The Church of Constantine identified closely with the imperial culture. Its structures benefited so much from this identification that it became the ally of the emperor and then, later on, of the state. As a result, the Church was unable to remain truly prophetic — it would have meant being critical of those expressions of society in which the Church saw itself mirrored. Some ecclesiastical trappings were inherited from the imperial court, including such banal things as genuflections and the kissing of bishops' rings — they certainly didn't come from the New Testament. The Church's preoccupation with retaining and exercising a kind of imperial power was a sign of how little it was truly prophetic. Because it was too much tied in with the temporal agenda of the state — and this is my thesis — the prophetic tradition which had developed with Moses and which Jesus had further perfected was jeopardized.

In my view, Vatican II represents a redawning of the prophetic vision, where the Church is able to be critical of society, where it is genuinely called to discern the signs of the times and judge them in terms of God's Reign.

* Fortress, 1978.

Leddy: Remi, you're talking about Vatican II as a prophetic moment in the Church, but it seems to me that what happened there was the cumulative effect of what many people had been saying over many years. Often those people were criticized and disenfranchised and silenced in their own lifetime. Even now we see parallels in Latin American theologians who are trying to restate the mission of the Church in terms of the option for the poor. They have been silenced because they are challenging the structure and the status quo. Only recently, Jesuit theologians were killed in El Salvador. Brazilian theologian Leonardo Boff was censured by the Vatican. So here is a real question: how does the Church deal with the prophetic element? I keep thinking that one of the reasons Vatican II has been so fragile is that prophetic voices were not welcomed earlier and listened to in greater depth. Even though we did finally hear what they were saying about the position of the Church, we didn't listen soon enough — even to people like Cardinal Newman.

De Roo: We couldn't hear Cardinal Newman. The Church wasn't ready.

Leddy: Well, my point is that we take consolation that somehow the truth always prevails, but sometimes it takes so long that by the time a message is heard it's almost out of date. Vatican II was trying to get us to see what is good in the modern world. I think that if we had done that sooner, we would now be more able to speak with credibility about the weaknesses of the modern vision — including the myth of progress and all the rest. The other thing that strikes me is that, for every theologian of the status of Yves Congar, who articulated such a challenge in the years prior to Vatican II, there must have been a hundred others who had an idea and wanted to say something but were afraid when they saw what was happening to those who had begun to think and speak in new ways. And this takes a terrible toll. People become cynical, subservient, shrivelled, and all this creative energy is lost to the Church.

Roche: I think that in the term "prophecy" we may have a word that means different things to the three of us, let alone to people generally. I'd like to attempt a point of entry as a layman, the only layman in this dialogue.

De Roo: Depending on your interpretation of canon law.

Leddy: Where does that leave me?

Roche: Well, the only non-ministerial — all right, I won't press the point.

Leddy: I'm quite content not to be classified as either "clergy" or "laity," by the way. Sometimes it's helpful not to fit any obvious category.

Roche: We'll save that discussion. But I do perhaps bring to this discussion of prophecy an unschooled approach. I approach this simply as a participant in a hurting world, a world in which there is an excessive amount of suffering brought about by unemployment, drugs, AIDS, the ramifications of the population explosion, intolerable amounts of human deprivation. We have an incessant militarism sucking up the resources, the energies of the world. I do not, however, bring to this discussion gloom and doom. In opening the Vatican Council, Pope John XXIII said (in effect), "Away with the gloom and doom and let's get on with the creativity." And I recognize that even in the areas I have just mentioned, there is a lot of creativity going into efforts to solve problems.

Right at the outset, I want to affirm that, if we live at the most dangerous moment in the history of the world as a result of what technology has brought about, we also live at the most creative moment. For me, the clash of these two overpowering themes, the negative and the positive, creates this moment. This is the dynamic of the modern world. You cannot fail to take account of the immensely negative as well as the creative, positive side of modernity. But when we put the two together, what is clear is that the scale of the problems is growing at a faster rate than the solutions. And my experience is that the problems of the hurting world are ethical problems. They have to do with how we are going to treat one another as human beings on this beautiful, blue, shimmering globe that we see spinning in space in the photographs sent back by the astronauts. And so I look for ethical leadership, leadership to bring a moral perspective to these complex problems.

Where should I look for this ethical leadership but to the Church? Yet what is the Church? Certainly not the Roman Catholic Church of Vatican City. I look to that community established by Christ that has always been described as a mystery. It's a communion — a communion held together in an institutional form. It was the institution that Vatican II sought to transform, to update, to renew, to cleanse, to purify. And there was much in Vatican II that did this, and that raised a hope, especially among those who were sensitive to the problems of suffering in the world, to the problems of disparities. It raised the hope that the Church would have the capacity to influence, to speak to the world. We had a marvelous manifestation of this very thing in the encyclical "Peace on Earth" (*Pacem in Terris*), which John XXIII issued about the time the Vatican Council was beginning. It's abundantly clear that that encyclical is addressed to the whole human family, not just the Catholic Church, and for that reason it has had a very great impact. *Pacem in Terris* set out a program for human rights, and it delineated those rights in a manner that had never been done before. It consigned colonialism, militarism and racism to the wastebaskets of history.

That encyclical, combined with "The Church in the Modern World" (*Gaudium et Spes*), raised up our hopes that we could continue God's creation and development here on earth, and that we could participate in all this as People of God with equality, you and I. This meant breaking down the barriers not only between you and me as Catholics, but between you and me as men and women, between you and me as Christians, Muslims, Hindus and so on. It was an electric, dynamic, dramatic moment.

My hope was that out of this would come a means or a motivation for the stimulation of stronger public policies that would triumph over the greed and exploitative patterns we've been mired in. My hope from Vatican II was not that this one event would suddenly create a miracle in the world, but that it would be a catalyst and stimulant and would widen out not just to the thirty-five hundred bishops who gathered at St. Peter's, but throughout the clergy, throughout the sisters, throughout the laity, into ecumenical dimensions, into the whole world. It had that potential. For me that was prophecy — that's what prophecy means to me. And I don't want to see it squelched by the reassertion of scholasticism, of institutionalism, of ecclesiasticism.

De Roo: I want to make two comments. First of all, Doug, with all my admiration for John XXIII, I'm a little less optimistic about *Pacem in Terris* than you are. Looking back now, we can see some of its limitations. We have moved well beyond it today. I'll give you illustrations. First, in my view, John XXIII's social analysis is too superficial. It proceeds largely along the line of the "sweet reason" of the Enlightenment philosophy.

And it does not — this is my second point — identify the historic cause of the poor as agents of liberation. To me, peace is more than a list of rights like those found in *Pacem in Terris*.

But I want to pick up your first point, your "thesis." In a constructive way, I want to take issue with it. I think prophecy has to move beyond the sphere of ethics. As long as we are dealing with ethical categories and ethical leadership, we are still talking to a great extent about means as opposed to meaning. We are trying to solve problems within a horizon that is too narrow. One of the reasons Vatican II was limited and weak (*Gaudium et Spes* now appears somewhat naive and excessively optimistic) is that it did not connect with the renewal of the prophetic imagination I mentioned earlier. It did not clearly establish the Reign of God as the ultimate criterion. It was still Church-centered, and to a great degree Euro-centered. Consequently, it was not able to offer a universal set of criteria by which ethical judgments could be made. Hence, people are still interpreting Vatican II in two quite different ways: the minimalist version and the maximalist version. The minimalist version emphasizes Vatican II's continuity with past teaching and practice. The maximalist version sees the Council opening up quite new ways of thought and action. Even the 1985 synod did not resolve that dilemma. Still, I would have to say that a theology that took conflict seriously did begin to emerge in 1985. In my view, we will need this conflictual theology, worked out in the light of the Reign of God, to give us the authority to speak ethically in a universal way that will not be rejected as just another theory.

Now, we do have a major problem here. How do we get into a new discourse with all the humanitarians, with all the so-called non-believers, with people of other religious traditions, on some of the fundamental issues that you raised, Doug — issues that are not soluble solely at the level of ethics? We have to go further and get to the deeper question about what it means to be human today. And until we get down to a discourse around what constitutes being human and what becoming more human means, we will not solve the problems of ethics.

Leddy: Maybe I can respond to both of you at this point. The thing that has struck me, as I look at my own experience, is that the prophetic cannot really be predicted or pinpointed. It shows up in unexpected places and people. This is why I'm glad — in spite of your minor slip, Doug — that we aren't talking in terms of the categories of bishops, priests, lay people. In my experience, there have been bishops who have been prophetic — like Romero, Hélder Câmara, Hume.

De Roo: And Seattle's Archbishop Hunthausen.

Leddy: Yes. And there have been prophetic priests and lay people. So really those categories are irrelevant in predicting where the prophetic is going to come from. It hasn't automatically come from lay people. It hasn't automatically come from the religious. And on the other hand, I see anti-prophetic tendencies in bishops, in priests, in sisters and in very right-wing Catholic laity.

We need a Church that exercises creative and life-giving power. But there exists within the Church, and in brief I would call it institutional sin, a system that disempowers the laity, disempowers priests. I'm from the Archdiocese of Toronto, and when I go to priests' meetings there, I come away depressed because I am listening to a group of men who are disempowered and who are therefore cynical and sub-servient. Because they know that if they say the wrong thing, they will be moved over and out and that will be the end of their so-called careers. The system disempowers bishops in the same way; there are many bishops who feel quite power-less. So there is something about the system that disempow-ers everyone in some way. And everyone contributes to that system of disempowering, and there is a sense in which many of us prefer it that way. It's not just a system imposed by some Vatican officials. We prefer to be powerless, we prefer to be irresponsible, rather than having to take on the ethical risk of exercising power in a creative and prophetic way. This is where we encounter something of the depth of sin. One of the most difficult things in the Church is to get people to want to move beyond the sense of powerlessness.

De Roo: May I raise a point about what you have just said? The point is this, that many prefer to remain powerless because our vision of reality, our model of the Church, is such that we have not yet awakened to the fact that we are called to empowerment. All of us.

Leddy: It's both. There are objective reasons why people feel powerless — the way the system operates makes people feel that way — but there is a deeper human mystery in that we sometimes want it to be that way. Even when we know it's wrong, and when we see an alternative. It's like the battered woman: she keeps being battered, she knows it's wrong but she keeps going back. Because the situation is bad but she knows it, it is at least predictable. For us to become a Church that exercises creative power — which is what's needed for the prophetic to take hold — we would all have to let go of a lot that is familiar. We would really have to take risks.

I think there has been so much coercive power in the Church that many people have reacted with a spirituality of powerlessness. And that's not what we need if, for the sake of the world, we are going to engage in the empowerment Doug is talking about.

Roche: I want to respond first to Mary Jo. I found your description of disempowerment in the Church very interesting and I thought it sounded just like the political structure I'm very familiar with. In other words, this disempowerment that you describe in priests, in bishops, is not peculiar to the Church. Those same feelings are found in politics and in government. Before the Vatican Council, power in the Church was in the form of a pyramid. Power in the Vatican II Church was conciliar, and I expected that sharing of power to continue in the post-conciliar Church, the sharing that comes out of the theological and scriptural basis of the Church as the People of God. My point is that the experience of disempowerment is not peculiar to the Church. Even people in political office can feel powerless.

I want to return to what Remi said in response to my emphasis on ethics. You said prophecy must move beyond ethics. Of course I agree. But what I want from the Church is a way of communicating the divinely infused humanity in the social order (or more precisely, perhaps, in the social *disorder*). In my practical experience, I am desperate for a leadership that will deal with the massive human problems that are worsening from the perspective of a true humanity. That's what prophecy is — the teaching of Jesus, unfettered by ecclesiasticism — and that's what I was searching for, and found, in Vatican II. So I look to the Church renewed, invigorated, to inject a strong ethical force into public policy formulation, so we can deal with these human problems in a way that I am sure God wants. That is our work. That's the prophetic message for me.

De Roo: I'd like to push that a little. As I perceive it, ethics is the fruit of culture. Ethics is the way a culture deals with its own issues. If you stay at that level, each culture has its own ethics. Once upon a time, slavery was acceptable. Women got the vote only recently. You see my point.

Leddy: I certainly do.

De Roo: So long as you have a universal culture, those things are generally accepted. For instance, as long as the European culture could pretend to dominate the world, you could have a standard of ethics that conformed to the European vision of reality. But the moment the culture begins to collapse, or the moment other cultures in the world begin to affirm themselves, they no longer accept the code of ethics of the alien culture. The Holy War is an example. American confrontation with the Arab nations is a classic example. Both of them claim to be right; both of them have God on their side. See my point?

Roche: Both of them are "right" in quotation marks, you mean.

De Roo: But each is right in its own terms because there is no higher common vision. This is precisely the problem.

Leddy: I think what Doug means by leadership is a leadership guided by vision, but by the *right* vision of humanity. And Remi, that's what you're saying: that ethics is determined by vision.

De Roo: A vision that goes beyond ethics.

Leddy: Where I would try to build on what you are saying is to suggest that often we have an experience of dirty power — in politics *and* in the Church. So we think of power as the power of control and the power of money — or the power of position, as it has been in the Church.

But there's another kind of power — and that's what I think you're getting at — that we have to believe in, and I think we've seen it in the last two years. We've seen it in Eastern Europe — the whole system fell apart. Now, some will argue that the economy had been terribly weakened. But it certainly didn't fall apart because the troops went in and blasted the hell out of the Russians. It didn't fall apart because there was a great worldwide boycott. It didn't fall apart because of all the men in grey suits. It fell apart because, in the end, people broke out of their little worlds of fear.

The Czech president, Václav Havel, says that both East and West live in materialistic cultures, and that we have lost faith in the power of an idea or a vision. There is a paradox in that the Church (and here I mean the institutional Church) squelches prophetic moments and can squelch people, yet it still carries a dangerous memory. It still holds a powerful vision that really is an alternative to the cultural vision which is crumbling.

Roche: I think it's probably good to focus on the word "vision" when considering prophecy. But yes, the Church does have a vision. It's been spelled out, for heaven's sake, in its social teaching for a hundred years.

Leddy: But it's not a vision if it doesn't command action and response. You are speaking of documents....

Roche: That's my point. Somehow the dynamic vision of Vatican II has been lost, mired in the institutional problems of administration and in certain ideological interpretations of Vatican II. I don't want us to get sidetracked into these ideological arguments. I feel a sense of urgency, given the state of the world and the potential of the Church to alleviate suffering.

De Roo: I want to pick up on what you just said, Doug — your comment that the Church does have a total world vision. I would say, since Vatican II, yes. Previous to Vatican II, no. And I want to explain why, briefly. Then I want to agree with what you said about the necessity of relaunching this dynamism.

To me, the sense of urgency comes from a rediscovery of the prophetic imagination. Prophecy in the Church puts us back into the context of eschatology. It says that the coming of Christ is imminent. It says Christ is actually present in history, so we are not speaking of some pie-in-the-sky; we are not speaking of something that's going to happen *eventually* as a result of evolution or progress. We have to be clear about this vision, which the Church didn't have before Vatican II.

To explain what I mean, let me mention two points that Avery Dulles deals with in his books *Models of Revelation* and *Models of the Church*.* In *Models of Revelation*, he places a strong accent on "inner experience," on the "dialectic presence of the Word," on the "new awareness of our relationship to God." In *Models of the Church*, he sees the Church as "sacrament," as "herald" and as "servant." Now, I would suggest that before Vatican II, the Church was locked into the model of the Church as institution. This was Bellarmine's classical theology, the theology I studied in seminary, in which the Church was, in a sense, perfect. The hierarchy was the totality of power and the hierarchy was justified in doing whatever it chose to do in its own good judgment. The Pope had all authority. The Pope's representatives could do anything they liked and nobody could question them. Because of that vision of the Church as institution, Vatican II came along and said, just a minute, this is too limited. It produces something doctrinaire which, pushed to the extreme, makes the Church a substitute for the Reign of God — if not actually for God. The Pope is placed on a pedestal, on a throne where he becomes almost divine. The extreme of that leads to a kind of idolatry. And Vatican II said, no, that's got to be corrected by an understanding of the Church as communion; by a recognition of the Church as the People of God, as herald and servant to the world. This is a very different vision.

* Doubleday, 1983 and 1974, respectively.

Leddy: But I think the vision of Vatican II was incomplete. You say it included all those models, but sometimes those models conflict. That wasn't clear at Vatican II. There is something about a prophetic movement that is inherently conflictual; it's in conflict with the status quo.

Roche: I know Remi wants to speak, and I'd like to encourage him by introducing the word "collegiality." Wasn't there something prophetic in the definition of collegiality in Vatican II? Wasn't that one of the great shifts in teaching that came out of the Council, the affirmation that the Pope would exercise his authority in concert with the College of Bishops? And the bishops would exercise their pastoral authority in a similar conjoining with members of their dioceses? And didn't all this mean that the Church as the People of God and the scriptural and eucharistic dimensions of the Church would be affirmed? That the old yoke of "control" would be broken in the new collegiality? And that the Spirit would be able to move in a Church more flexible, less rigid, more responsive, more pluralistic? You see, even as my mind goes back into all that, I find myself excited by the potential of such a Church. We've got to get that vision back. We can't lose it. We can't lose all that potential.

De Roo: Yes, collegiality was the major turning-point. I think one of the reasons collegiality was given so much attention was that the Council consisted primarily of bishops so it touched them more directly. But deeper than collegiality between bishops and the Pope was the rediscovery of the People of God, and ministries emerging not out of ordination but out of baptism. That was another major turning-point. The almost unanimous voice showed that the Spirit was on the side of those who spoke for collegiality. That to me is symbolic because it is breaking away, officially, from the institution model and moving into those other dimensions of communion that are part of collegiality. Because communion emphasizes not structures but relationships. Yes, that was very important.

Leddy: Yet I think the model of the Church as communion finds it very difficult to deal with conflict. The sense of communion is consensus, harmony. Communion mitigates against group conflict, but conflict can in the end lead to change and empowerment. It's very disempowering when people say, "I object," and are then marginalized for disturbing the harmony, for disrupting the community.

De Roo: Yes — unless you push the notion of communion to its ultimate meaning. Because I am in relationship to God as a creature made in the image of the Trinity, I have certain rights, powers and privileges that no one can take away from me. So yes, we have to open up the communion model and acknowledge that it has to include conflict.

Roche: I would like to suggest that our problem is not that the "People of God" are all gung ho and ready to go, and are simply being blocked by those in authority. There is a great sluggishness in the Church, an inertia. Lots of people are rather frightened by great concepts like communion and collegiality. And I can make my point by giving a very homely example — something that happened recently.

I was in a church where the priest was giving a homily at Mass. I wouldn't say it was the most inspired sermon I'd heard in my life, but I wouldn't call it the worst. All of a sudden, there arose from midpoint in the congregation the voice of a man who started criticizing the homily and, by indirection, the priest. It was clear that he wasn't inebriated or irrational or crazy. He was a serious man expressing a serious concern. He was asking why the priest didn't preach about social justice. He said he had been in the parish six or seven years and had never heard a sermon on social justice, about the meaning of Jesus' teaching applied to that very community. He had a valid point. But the congregation was mostly scandalized at the effrontery of this chap publicly complaining to the pastor about his preaching. That showed me that, from the pastoral point of view, there are traffic zones out there! Most people are still treating the Church not as a dynamic center of prophecy but as a service station to which they go for refueling and a little personal comfort. I'm not sneering at sacramental grace — God help us all, we need it. But it seems to me that, in the judgment of many priests, providing a comfort zone is about all the traffic will bear.

Leddy: Well, yes — I almost totally agree. But your average Catholic, if there is such an animal (and I doubt it, somehow), is hit in a very simple way by the kind of issues we are talking about. Let's go back to the issue of women in the Church — the average Catholic asks, why can't girls serve as altar boys do? Having altar girls is a matter of common sense.

Roche: The answer is very simple — they might get the idea that they want to be priests. That's why they can't be altar girls!

Leddy: My point is that most Catholics aren't all that gung ho about intricate theological issues, but that doesn't mean they're asleep. They may not ask these questions that probe deeply into matters of justice, but they ask simpler, more immediate questions.

De Roo: Just for the record, the problem of altar girls is a false problem. I'm not saying that to put you down, and I'll come back to it later. But at this point I want to come back to Doug's fellow who protested from the pew. Without wanting to judge the particulars of that situation — which I'm not in a position to do — I agree that the man may have a point. To ask that the meaning of Jesus' words and ministry be related to our own lives and our own communities is hardly an unreasonable request.

In that connection, I want to mention a new book by Carlos Mesters called *The Defenseless Flower.** It tells of illiterate peasants in the Third World who have rediscovered the Word of God because they have been given back the Bible, to which people like them have not had access for a long time. In the absence of clerical leadership, they are rereading the Scriptures with a new set of eyes, and hearing them with a new set of ears. They are confronting the Word of God in the face of their experience of poverty, and putting those two things together is very much in the prophetic tradition. What I am getting at, really, is the question of nourishment. There are many people who say it is not enough for us to be "sacramentalized," however crucial the sacramental aspect of our worship. The sacraments are a celebration of the Word, a celebration of the Story, but a lot of people are fed up with sermons that tell them how to behave themselves. They want to be nourished with the Word of God, and the way they will be nourished by the Word of God is by retelling the Story in such a way that their own story relates to the biblical story.

Again we are back to the prophetic tradition. When that man said, "How about talking about social justice?" he was touching a key point. In effect, he was asking about making a link with the Word of God instead of just talking about personal morality or about how we administer the sacraments. I think we are going to hear an increasing number of lay people express their frustration with the limited quality of the sermons they hear, and it's partly because we are not preaching the true, the real Story. We are not getting back to the Scriptures and we are not putting preaching in the context of the

* Orbis, 1989.

Reign of God. We are too much into the nitty-gritty of how to run a parish, how best to celebrate the sacraments, how to set up catechism programs or meet the practical needs of all sorts of organizations.

Leddy: I wonder in retrospect whether one of the most revolutionary statements of Vatican II was that Catholics can read the Scriptures and make them their own. Because before that, reading the Bible was something Protestants did. That change may have been one of Vatican II's most significant achievements.

Another thing — I think we've been pretty clear about what institutional Church structures can do to a prophetic spirit. But maybe it's not nearly as bad as what the dominant culture does to an alternative vision. In the Church it's obvious what happens in these confrontations, and yet when you study those who are considered prophetic or radical — say someone like Dan Berrigan — they are people who are sustained by the biblical story, by sacraments and by discipline. In my experience, the most long-term radical people in areas of justice and peace are religiously committed and even, in certain respects, traditional people. They are not New Age fluffies. Also, I'm talking of people who have more than just an intellectual view of social justice. I mean people whose imaginations have been transformed by another set of symbols and stories.

And this brings me to another point. What I see happening in subtle ways — and it's almost as debilitating for the prophetic dimension as anything Church officials themselves might do — is what I would call the professionalization of ministry. This happens to clergy, to religious lay people — anybody who gets involved in ministry in more than a passing way. I find it interesting that the ministry or clergy always follow the dominant model of their society. It used to be the feudal lord, and then it was the Renaissance prince, and now I think it's the professional. People have to get a theology degree and pass their exams and all that. And unfortunately, lay people are taking this up. Only if they have done theology courses are they "qualified." And by the time they get their certificates or degrees, they have been so enculturated into the professional, managerial ethos that any prophetic dimension of their call has been neutralized. There has got to be a better path, between the extremes of learning the "truth" so it can be disseminated with authority from on high, or speaking only out of your own little experience. The professional model, which is highly individualistic and very competitive, teaches people nothing about community and nothing about the practices of reading the Scriptures and prayer, practices that nourish the prophetic imagination.

De Roo: May I just link what you have said with the institutional model of the Church? Because it's too easy to slip back into that model rather than the "servant," "herald" or "communion" model. And sacramental teaching obviously lends itself very readily to the institutional model, because of the way we have defined sacraments as administrative acts or "things." Couple all that with the Enlightenment's emphasis on the purely rational and the whole view of the Church becomes a head trip — a rational, institutional model.

Leddy: Double whammy.

De Roo: There is a double whammy, precisely, for the people who fall into the professional, managerial model. If I have my diploma on the wall, I'm the authority.

Leddy: Here's a concrete example. I've talked to people who say, I really want to work for social justice, I've learned about this and I want to be involved in the Church, but I have to have a job that pays enough that I can have a computer, a library, subscriptions to the right periodicals, memberships in various groups, support to attend conferences — because without all this I won't be effective. Something's wrong here. Those are all helpful but they are not prerequisites to doing something. That's another subtle way in which people get incapacitated.

De Roo: The best answer to that, of course, is the Raging Grannies, who claim no professional status. No diplomas, no books, no jobs, but ready to put hearts and bodies on the line.

Leddy: Yes! I'm all for learning, you know — I want to be clear about that. But the capacity for leadership or power for change is as much mitigated by the culture as it is by the Church. The cultural norm is that only those with professional credentials are able to deal with social problems.

Roche: As we approach the end of the discussion, I'd like to focus once again on what we mean by prophecy. Does prophecy tell us about things timeless in the midst of dynamic cultural change? Is it something that primarily calls for personal integrity and strengthens our own relationship with God? Or is it something that sends us outward in a caring, collaborative manner to improve the human condition, or the condition of humans? Doubtless, both dimensions of prophecy are found today. I'm not overly fond of labels, but as a kind of shorthand I'll say that the conservative element in the Church seems to seize upon the internal relationship of the human being to God, while the more liberal element reaches outward in social concerns.

Mary Jo, you suggested at one point that, in the liberal interpretation of Vatican II, we were "accepting the modern world," and that's why the conservatives were resisting — they were worried that liberals were too ready for the Church to accommodate secular modernity. But in fact the liberal perspective, of reaching outward, goes back to Jesus himself, who reached out to the poor, to the disenfranchised, to those who were discriminated against in society. For me, the prophetic message of Jesus is to reach outward, not just upward.

De Roo: I accept everything you say, Doug. I think it reflects your initial approach, and I think it's valid. But I want to add to that another dimension which I think we are in danger of neglecting when we talk about prophecy. I suggest that what you just told us about focusing on prophecy as either personal interiority or outreach to humanity, and citing the example of Jesus, still represents only that aspect of prophecy which is *human* initiative. And I want to bring back into focus the other dimension of prophecy, which I think is even more important — *divine* initiative. That's why I keep coming back to the idea that we have to tell the Story. Real prophecy is not primarily what human beings or prophets themselves have done. The fullness of prophecy lies in the initiative of God sending into history the person of Jesus. His is not just human compassionate outreach. It is also that revolutionizing and upsetting presence of the divine that changes the course of history. It gives history a totally new meaning. It makes it possible to have a vision which is beyond all ethics, and according to which all ethics, coming out of whatever culture, are ultimately to be judged.

Let's go a step further and connect this with a much larger international and intercultural dialogue around the concept of the human. It is divine prophecy, divine initiative which ultimately reveals the full meaning of the human.

Leddy: I want to respond to Doug's point about conservatives and liberals. I think it's always important to qualify those terms, because I know of some conservatives who, out of deep commitment to the Gospel, are very worried that the Church has sold out to the culture, has been co-opted by a culture that uses the Church for its own purposes. So I do see room in the Church for a good, spirited conservative who, out of commitment to the Gospel, really engages with the liberal. There can be honest conflict between people who have commitment to the Gospel but disagree over a basic assessment of the world around them. I think that's a good conflict. And it will give light.

But then there is another conflict which is just a religiously baptized repetition of the liberal–conservative debate in the culture. And the press gets so interested in this. People call me up all the time, they want to have a confrontation between a conservative cardinal and a liberal nun. It's great media but it just plays out the drama of the culture — it goes nowhere. It's a dead end and it will never give light because it isn't motivated by a commitment to the Gospel. You can tell when people have been taken over by the Gospel. You may not agree with them, but you know that what they are saying is coming out of this essential commitment. In these encounters or conflicts, something worthwhile is going on. But the other kind of liberal–conservative debate is increasingly boring. As far as I'm concerned, for the sake of the Gospel, we must all make a choice about what questions to discuss and what questions to put aside. Some questions aren't worth our time and energy. They have no connection with anything prophetic.

✛ III ✛

WOMEN IN THE CHURCH:
UNFINISHED REVOLUTION

*L*eddy: It may seem a strange place to start, but I want to begin this reflection on women by talking not about Mary but about Joseph. Joseph is often presented as the model father of the family, the model worker and all that. But it strikes me that he was really the paradigm of a man who is confronted by a woman who has had an experience that doesn't fit into his categories of understanding. Mary was telling him that something new was happening to her that didn't fit into either her categories or his. This was a very scary situation. But the thing that is remarkable about Joseph is that he trusted her — he trusted her with something new that he didn't understand. I have also been reflecting on the fact that, while Joseph has always been an important figure in the mind of the Church, none of the popes has ever chosen the name Joseph. I think that's interesting.

Anyway, what I'm suggesting is that the experience of women in our time, at least of women in the Western world, was not understood at Vatican II. It wasn't part of it. I think we would all agree that the experience of women in the last twenty-five years, or more, is dramatically new. And the new insight, which — let's be clear about this — has come more from the secular world, is that women are equal in every way. Not that they are necessarily the same as men, but that there is a basic human equality. Now, I think this insight has roots in a biblical vision, but that's another point. What I feel certain about is that this insight is not going to go away — because it is so fundamentally true. It's true in terms of the Gospel. It's a consciousness that has entered as a wedge of truth into the minds of enough people that it cannot be lost, no matter what happens. It's like when Galileo said the earth was round — people kept saying, it's flat, it's flat. But once that basic insight was evident, it couldn't be denied for ever.

I think the problem today is that women in the Church — and I'm going to limit myself for the moment to North America and Europe — are in a kind of schizophrenic position. Increasingly they are treated as equals in society, but not in the Church. There has been some effort in the Canadian Church and the American Church to address this, but it has been patchwork and, in some cases, mere tokenism. If equality is really taken seriously, it will mean a radical restructuring in the Church. People know that, and it's the source of much of the resistance. I think the most serious pastoral question is, how long can this schizophrenic situation go on? Admittedly, feminists are not the majority of the Church, but I don't think women can live with this situation much longer. I think of my niece and cousins in high school and elementary school; they can't fathom the contradiction between their public, secular experience and their Church experience. And I believe that unless the Church addresses this soon, and in a very fundamental way, we are going to lose not just one generation of women but many generations. I see it as comparable to the worker-priest crisis in post-war France, when, because the Vatican decreed an end to the experiment of priests working in factories, a whole class of people was lost to the Church. And there are other examples historically. Terrible mistakes can be made and whole groups of people can be alienated, and it simply isn't good enough to say, "Well, the Church will go on." More than that, as long as this basic injustice continues, it corrodes the soul of the Church.

One of the things that has bothered me the most is a kind of theological prostitution — a justifying of the inequality of women; all the elaborate arguments against ordination, against altar girls, all that kind of thing. If the problem is that the Church is not quite "ready" for such changes, I wish people would put it in those terms. But using the Scriptures and theological arguments to justify untenable practices is destroying the soul of the Magisterium.* I also feel it's a terrific loss for women because I don't think there's any better place to go. Many women who move outside the churches end up forming separatist religious groups or becoming liberal, secular professionals. This isn't really — in my view — an adequate alternative.

I've thought a lot about the reasons for the resistance to women in the Church, and despite the mountains of "rational" argument defending the traditional place of women, I've come to the conclusion that the true reason for resistance isn't rational. It has to do with fear of the emotional power of women. Both women and men have this fear because of the way the family has been structured. The woman has been the source of emotional, affective power. It has been hers to give or take away, because the father was more distant — at work. And the thought of having women in positions of power in the Church is, for that reason, really frightening. So it's not so much a dismissing of women; it's an actual fear of them, a fear of the power in the mother image.

* the teaching authority of the Church.

Roche: I want to begin with an apology: that Remi and I conducted a dialogue twenty-five years ago without a female perspective made our discussions gravely deficient. But in the intervening years, as a husband and a father, I do think I can say I've learned a few things! When I look back to the time of Vatican II and remember how much resistance there was to having an internationally renowned woman like Barbara Ward address a post-conciliar synod, I realize how terribly the Church has lost by excluding women. Excluding women from the priesthood is, of course, a central issue, but for me it's just the tip of the iceberg. Underneath the surface is a residue of paternalism and exclusion and — I would accept your point — a fear of women that has permeated the Church. So the issue as I see it is not just women priests, although women clearly should be eligible for the priesthood, but women as fully accepted "People of God." I am unable to understand how the Church can on the one hand affirm the equality of all at baptism and on the other hand exclude women from the ordained ministry. But I agree that there is indeed a fear of women, and I think that fear is rooted in a fear of sexuality.

Leddy: But I'm saying something different, Douglas. I'm talking about the emotional power — potentially the controlling power — of the "mother." There are many men who react deeply against that power. And women react against it too.

Roche: Well, I'll reserve my point. I think a fear of sexuality *is* involved.

De Roo: Mary Jo, you have opened up a dialogue in depth on this subject. I think this conversation could be a sign of hope to people that these things can be talked about openly. And they must be. But I would like to broaden the topic and point out that, at their very important meeting in Puebla in 1979, the Latin American bishops recognized that women are *doubly* oppressed. They were referring, of course, to illiterate peasants, but I think it's important that these official statements have been made, and very important that they be generally known. Although it's true that women were largely absent from the Vatican Council until the close, *Lumen Gentium* and other conciliar and post-conciliar documents describe the reality of God as transcending gender. This gives us a strong basis on which we can set aside any comparisons of men and women which imply the subordination of one to the other. Also — thanks in great part to women scholars — we are rediscovering powerful images of women in the Scriptures. I had the opportunity some time ago to be part of a retreat on precisely this question, and had to do a bit of homework, so I have a whole series of examples — birthing, nursing, feeding, protecting and so on. All of these provide excellent grounds for the use of inclusive language in theology, prayer and worship. But further, I want to put on record here, because I am very proud of them, some words from a statement of the Quebec bishops on the liberation of women:

Whatever our situation may be and from whatever standpoint we may observe this issue, the liberation of women is unquestionably a sign of our times. If we use the word "liberation" it is because women have, in fact, been bound and oppressed. This liberation has neither occurred everywhere nor been completed where begun. It is therefore a Christian issue consistent with the fundamental teachings of Jesus Christ. The liberation of women is a challenge and a responsibility for men as well as women, for the hierarchy as well as the whole people of God. The clergy as well as the laity. Everyone working together must actualize in this world [these] values proposed by the Gospel....

This is a deliberate statement made by a large sector of the Canadian episcopate, in full knowledge that it would be controversial and would probably cause shock waves in certain quarters. To me that is a very hopeful sign.

Leddy: I appreciate what you are both saying, and I agree with you, but I don't feel — with notable exceptions, Remi — that the leadership of the Church recognizes that this feminist revolution is just beginning. It has a long way to go, and in some ways, therefore, it is very messy. For instance, there is a kind of feminism right now that is fundamentally reactive: if men do this, we do that. I think the abortion debate is typical of this. There is a strong feminist reaction to a very oppressive patriarchal system that has treated women's bodies as men's property, and women are now saying, "No! My body is *my* property!" But both positions are encased in the private-property view of the body as a possession — which is regressive.

This reactive attitude is going to be with us for some time and the churches have got to tolerate the mess, the excesses. In this conversation I am able to be calm. But I do have my angry moments. I am dealing here with two pleasant men, but you know I have been so insulted, insulted by the gross responses of some Church leaders. So anger is part of this unfinished revolution. And we have to grant a legitimacy to the anger, to see it as fueling creativity. It's very important to enter into the feminist discussion. There are factions, there are dialogues, there are debates. There are a lot of women trashing women. At the same time, some of the most creative thinking going on in North America is being done by feminists — on basic questions about the view of the person, the view of society, the vision of the world. This thinking has enormous promise for the Church, if it's taken seriously.

The other thing I want to talk about is the need to be *with* women who are going through crises of faith. These crises are a kind of dark night where some images of God, *many* images of God which exclude women, no longer hold meaning. Some people become bereft and profoundly confused. And one thing that I don't appreciate — and many people do this, Church people do it — is hearing women's concerns dismissed as merely middle-class worries about jobs and inclusive language, and being told that what we should be concerned about is the poor. I think this kind of put-down is something we should not engage in. I have heard the liberation theologian Gustavo Gutiérrez speak very movingly about how his mother was the one who put him through theology and worked as a cleaning woman without a husband. No one in Latin America has written more powerfully about the oppression of the poor, but he also knew in his skin what the oppression of women was about. So I think we shouldn't engage in disparaging the concerns of women.

The good news — and I don't know how this is going to pan out in the churches — the good news is that this is all spawning a male spirituality. In his latest book, *Iron John*,* Robert Bly is saying that men who were conscious of the first wave of feminism often became wimps, thinking they had to accept everything and not be so assertive. Bly says no, it's not that, we men need to reach into the depths of our own passion and energy, rather than deny them. So it's like a recasting of sexual roles in society, which I think is just wonderful. It's going to take seventy-five or a hundred years, but it has such promise! If only we could see all the mess and the anger and the excesses as something promising and hopeful for the world, and for the Church, because the change has the potential to transform human relationships.

Of course, the burden of the past lies heavy here. We are talking not just about ongoing sexism in the Church but about women who have been abused. The statistics are stunning — some studies say four out of ten women. As a result, a

* Addison-Wesley, 1990.

deep personal woundedness gets unleashed when the question of women is discussed. So, Remi, while I am grateful for the Quebec bishops' statement and other things that have been done, and sometimes done with tremendous courage, I don't think we can afford a "go slow" approach in this. We have mentioned the ordination of women. Do you know, I'm not even interested. I'm not interested in the priesthood for men or women, the way it is now, with the structure it has — so for me it's not an engaging question. Now, that's a terrible thing to say, because women are supposed to be encouraging men to go into the priesthood. But I think there are a lot of women who just say, why?

Roche: They are not encouraging their sons to go into the priesthood.

Leddy: Not encouraging their sons or friends or whomever. And it used to be a great thing to become a priest. But I know that, after conversations with certain Church officials in which I, as a woman, have felt deeply insulted, I have just felt I would not engage in conversations with such people again. It would be beneath me. Perhaps that sounds arrogant, but that's what I felt. I felt they were small, frightened men.

Roche: Again, I think we ought to remember that, while we are talking about a problem in the Church, it also exists in society as a whole. The problems of discrimination against women and violence against women are well known, and we ought not to single out the Church as the sole culprit in holding women down. Society has done that aplenty. When I first went into the House of Commons in 1972, I think there were only six or seven women in the place. Now there are about forty (which is still far below proportional representation). It's only in recent years that women have been able to get a breakthrough into most professions. So I see the resistance to women in the Church as being connected to the discrimination against women in society as a whole, based on cultural values of previous times. That being said, the integrity of the Vatican II documentation on who we are as a Church and a People of God cannot permit this discrimination to go on.

Leddy: I think I should say that I'm under no illusion that if women were treated as equals in the Church and society everything in the Church and society would automatically be better. I really don't think it's wise for women to indulge in the romantic notion that they are more sensitive than men and morally better, because that's saying we have to be better than men to be treated justly — it's no more than a variation of the old pedestal problem. What will happen, I think, is that as women exercise more power we will become aware of the particular forms of female destructiveness. And that will be another awareness of our equality.

Roche: Regardless of that, the Church loses a lot by not having the full participation of women. Let me digress for a second to tell you a little anecdote. It's well established that women cannot preach a homily during the Mass at the time normally appointed, right after the Gospel.

De Roo: That applies to all lay people, not just women. It's a false problem.

Roche: You're right, of course. But let me just complete my anecdote, anyway. I was in a church the other day that has a woman leading the choir, and I noticed that they had her speaking in introducing the first reading. And what she gave was the equivalent of a homily. After the Gospel, the priest just spoke for a minute or two. In other words, it looked like a transparent effort to make an end run around the rule whereby women (all right, lay people) can't give a homily. Of course, the fact that the pastor wanted this woman to speak was in itself a very positive sign.

Leddy: I want to hear women express their views — mind you, I don't want to back into the position that a woman will preach well just because she's a woman. What matters is who she is as a person, as a Christian. Because we could get a Maggie Thatcher, and I'm not too keen to hear her!

Roche: Well, gender is no determinant of wisdom — or of sensitivity and compassion. I've worked in the disarmament field and in government with women, who are alleged by certain people to be more caring, nurturing and sensitive to the whole war question, but some of them turned out to be more hawkish than men — and I've worked with men who were far more sensitive than many women. Yet I still come back to my general principle here: while recognizing that gender is a poor guide to how a person is going to react, I believe there are qualities in feminine psychology, perhaps of cultural origin, that are more conducive to the sensitizing, or humanizing, of public policy. I see that in the political and social order, so it seems to me that male predominance in the religious realm not only is arrogant but also deprives the Church of a tremendous input from half the People of God.

De Roo: May I just come back to your previous point about the homily? I said it was a false problem because the rule from canon law applies to all laity. But I want to reflect on that. Why worry about whether it's the homily? Instead of taking the canon law approach, let's take the pastoral approach. Why are we together to worship in the first place? It's to witness to our common faith as a community. Nothing in canon law says we can't have sharing of faith reflections. Women can do that as well as men. And whether it happens right after the Gospel or elsewhere, what's the difference? You offered the example of a woman giving a commentary on the ecclesial reading — fine and good. But let's take a further step. Let's restructure our liturgies to be more flexible so that the whole community — both women and men — has a chance to share faith reflections around the Word of God, and not worry or quarrel over the term "homily."

Leddy: I think that's a creative option. I actually suggested it at one parish where women had been banned from preaching. The interesting thing was that people didn't want to. It was too much work to engage in that kind of thinking and reflecting.

Roche: Homilies aside, the Church is not being the "People of God" when women are denied full recognition and respect. We have to confront and understand our fears and our resistance to the new role of women. The relationship between the sexes has changed and we have to come to terms with the new order. We have to enter the struggle. The question is not going to go away.

✠ IV ✠

SEX THE CATHOLIC WAY

*R**oche:*** Vatican II defined marriage as a covenant relationship which entails the building of a community of life and love. Further, it offered a clear interpretation of sexual intercourse as integral to the communication of love within such a relationship. In other words, it did not see sexual intercourse as a necessary evil or something designed for procreation purposes only. It saw it as integral to the communication of love. And this changed view of sexual intercourse has profound consequences. It not only affirms the integrity of marital communication but it gives dignity to that which is given in creation. Sexuality is seen as an essential and central characteristic of our humanity. All this represents a very positive step forward, something that in my view is totally consonant with the view of who we are in the Church — the People of God in communion with each other, not just institutionally associated with each other. Out of this view comes responsible parenthood.

As a sixty-one-year-old man, the father of five children, I don't think I'll be viewed as speaking with a vested interest if I argue the legitimacy of birth control. Of course, the Church's official documentation on this question takes another position — one I think is an inappropriate use of ecclesiastical authority. In 1968, the Canadian bishops, at some risk, issued a statement that affirmed the use of informed conscience on the question of birth control. The statement was welcomed by the laity in Canada — it relieved many of an intolerable burden of conscience — and it pointed a new direction for the whole Church. Unfortunately, the views expressed in that statement did not ultimately prevail in the Vatican, and I think that was a terrible mistake. Just as the Church had to change its view on Galileo, so too the idea that was inherent in pre-conciliar Church teaching, that this bountiful earth could support an unlimited number of human beings, has surely got to change. The world's population has doubled since 1950, and a billion more people are going to be added in the 1990s. This is a critical planetary problem that the Church absolutely must address.

Overpopulation aside, the question of human sexuality raises a whole series of issues: married priests, women priests, divorce, homosexuality, sexual abuse, violence toward women and so on. All these matters have to be on the Catholic agenda.

De Roo: As a bishop I face enormous pastoral questions in this area. Missionaries have long been aware that the meaning of sexuality and marriage is conditioned by culture and history, as well as by the different stages in human development. Sexuality doesn't mean the same thing for a teenager as it does for an octogenarian, even though it is important at all stages because we are all sexual beings. And the understanding of marriage and sexuality is not the same, in parts of Africa, for instance, as it is in North America.

But what I want to indicate is an openness in Vatican II to the complexities and cultural variations that pertain to this issue. In view of those variations, I have to put the question: can we have one universal practice, or universal discipline, that can be equally understood, accepted and followed by a variety of peoples in different parts of the world?

This question is linked, I think, to a deeper issue which takes us to the level of doctrine, and which was touched on by Vatican II. For lack of a better term, I will call it the Cardinal Newman question: how do we relate the evolution of the Church's teaching and the concept of informed conscience? And a further dimension we have to keep in mind is that offered by Thomas Kuhn in his book *The Structure of Scientific Revolutions*.* Kuhn explains how the commonly accepted paradigm of knowledge, the knowledge or insights that are taken for granted as constituting the corpus of common sense in a community, can suddenly, for reasons often not very clear, undergo a huge change. Society moves to a whole new way of living and understanding. There is something of a parallel here — certainly not an exact parallel — between what happens in science and what happens in morality and even theology. I think this bears on an understanding of where we are going on the question of sexuality and male-female relationships; it's probably correct to see it in terms of such a paradigm shift. This means that the old rational arguments don't quite fit and the old forms of discipline don't seem to apply.

Leddy: I'd like to take off from this idea of a paradigm shift. My sense is that we can't really deal with this question of sex, or sexuality, outside a larger interpretive framework. Sex is not isolated, independent of the rest of life. It's related to meaning, to how we see life, how we view the world and ourselves in the world. When I was growing up, I never really encountered what people think of as the Church's traditional teaching about marriage. Was this a misconception — this rigid, limited view of marriage? I

* University of Chicago Press, 1970.

don't remember it. I know I've read it in books since then, but it wasn't really my experience.

I do understand, intellectually, that there was a view of sexuality and gender that was tied into a view of a natural law, a view that there was a natural way of doing things for men and for women, and that sex was about having babies, and that you shouldn't interfere with the process of nature: all that was seen to be part of a natural order. Now, when this question of birth control was being discussed in the sixties, I decided to consult somebody I thought knew something about it. So I talked to my dad, who was the chief of staff of a large Catholic hospital, and very concerned in his conscience to follow the teachings of the Church on medical ethics. I asked him what he thought about the Church's position on birth control. He said, "Well, I'm really not sure, but I know this — the reasons given are just terrible." He put it this way: "As I understand it, the reasons given are that you can't interfere with the course of nature. Mary Jo, everything we do in this hospital interferes with the course of nature. If they're right, nothing we're doing makes sense, because every single person here is being helped by interference with the course of nature." I never forgot that. The whole view of the natural law was being challenged by what was best in modern technology and know-how, and by people like my father. I think the vast majority of people have seen such intervention as a good thing. It has made human life better. So when the Church has used the reason that we can't do things that interfere with nature as a basis for its proscription of birth control, it just hasn't made sense to people.

Now the statistics say that habits of birth control and sexual practice are just about the same among Catholics as in the rest of society. So there's a set of official teachings but meanwhile Catholics are basically doing what everybody else is doing. They have simply decided to do what they think is best. That's a fact. I also have to say — and I think I go to Mass quite a bit — that I don't hear anybody speaking about sexuality from the pulpit. I can't recall the last time I heard a sermon on birth control or sexual morality. I think the clergy are running shy on this because they know the laity have criticized them, as celibates, for speaking about these issues.

This is rather a sad situation because what we are left with is a kind of privatized morality in one area of life, while we are calling for a greater social consciousness in other areas. I also think it's very serious when Church teaching is simply ignored. We really have to look at the question of coherency. It's unfortunate that we have reached a point of such incredulity that priests are reluctant to speak about issues of sexuality, because this is a place where there is a great deal of pain in people's lives. Jean Vanier has written very movingly about this, that the core woundedness of many people is situated in their sexuality — the abuse of it, a lack of integration, a hurt that needs healing.

I have one more comment on Remi's idea of a paradigm shift: I think we are moving into yet another paradigm shift, where the whole ecological consciousness is beginning to question how we interfere with nature, in our bodies or in the natural processes of the earth.

Roche: Let me come back to a point you touched on, which is for me very important. You said that it's not good when part of the teaching is ignored, and that you worried about having a privatized morality on the one hand and a concern that the Church be clear about its social teaching on the other. I wonder how the Spirit works. Does the Spirit only work by infusing the Magisterium of the Church in its conciliar moments? Does the Spirit only roam around up there on the mountain top, infusing the ecclesiastical leadership, or does it also work down in the valleys? Can it be said of these many

Catholics who are making their own decisions on this question that they may actually be reflecting the Spirit? Maybe they reflect a more profound understanding of sexuality than is found in certain other quarters.

Leddy: What concerns me about the contradiction between official teaching and popular practice is this: religion presents a whole vision of life, not just bits and pieces of teaching. So where there is massive incoherence in one area of life, the wholeness of the vision suffers, fragments.

Roche: But the change *is* happening. Vast numbers are ignoring the teaching of the Church. So I'm raising a question of how the Spirit works in the Church.

De Roo: Doug, I want to pick up on your mountains and valleys image, because it makes me very uncomfortable. I want to go back to what the Council taught us in *Lumen Gentium*, that the Spirit infuses all members of the Church and the Spirit moves where it will. As a result, all members of the Church have to make responsible decisions. I recognize the political malaise of the moment, with orders coming from the center, and I struggle with that. But I want to get at the question that lies behind what you were saying about where the Spirit works.

It's the question of how decisions are reached and how people's consciences are formed. Pope John Paul put out a peace message on the first of January 1991, on the question of freedom of conscience. He talked about the necessity of informed conscience, because if conscience is not informed in relation to truth and divine law, it really expresses nothing but personal preference. When the Canadian bishops spoke in 1968, they talked about a balance of values in conflict. They understood that married couples could not, under all circumstances, maintain all values, so they accepted a priority in values, something like the Vatican Council's acceptance of a "hierarchy of truths." Given that understanding, one can say that conscience is formed not only on the basis of theoretical principles, but also out of lived experience. So what we are looking at is a kind of pastoral evolution.

Let me give another example of a major change in Church law relating to marriage. For the first time in history, the new code of canon law acknowledges psychological factors — psychological capacity — in establishing whether or not a marriage was truly constituted. This is a change of a pretty fundamental order. Place that alongside other things that came out of the Council — for instance, the idea that the scientific exposition of moral theology has to be better nourished by the Scriptures and the Christ story — and you begin to see, from yet another perspective, that something has to change.

Well, my point is that it's already changing, although the Church's legislation has not yet caught up with it. I believe the laity are moving with that understanding. They have gifts, they have charisms built out of their experience. They too relate to the mystery of Christ and to the Scriptures. They too are aware of the modern sciences, so they no longer tolerate decisions made for them in abstraction from their lived experience.

Roche: You put this in hopeful terms, in terms that suggest a shortening of the conflict between a questionable use of hierarchical authority and the work of the Spirit in the whole Church, in the People of God.

De Roo: Let me come back for a moment to this question of legislation. You asked about how decisions are made. Then you went on to say that there's a process taking place among the people that is ahead of the legislation. One reason the issue of sexuality, as it surfaces in the birth-control issue, is so important is because it's directly connected to Vatican II's affirmation of a collegial Church. In effect, Pope Paul VI unilaterally overruled what is now known to be a majority opinion in his Expert Commission on the birth-control question. It recommended to the Pope that contraception be allowed. In overruling that recommendation, he appears to have diminished the advances of Vatican II. His example reinforced the view, in the curial element around him, that the principle of co-responsibility which was at the heart of Vatican II could be not only diminished but dismissed. And the fact that the issue was birth control left many people in real torment, because they don't want to be at odds with the Church but they just can't accept the Pope's veto. And the silence from the pulpits in their own parish churches does nothing to resolve the dilemma.

Leddy: Well, I feel a bit like the worldly cynic here. I'm very impressed, Remi, with your tremendous affirmation of the Spirit in the laity, and of their growing Christian awareness. But I'm also impressed with the way you are affirming the power of the hierarchy. *Power* of the hierarchy, I'm saying — not their authority, but their power, their influence. And yet as I read the statistics — you know, Andrew Greeley in the United States and Reginald Bibby in Canada, and the others — I'm not saying Catholic practice *is* changing, I'm saying it *has* changed, and it has been changed for ten years.

De Roo: It was Doug who was emphasizing the power of the hierarchy in our earlier discussions.

Leddy: I know. And saying that it still wields all this influence. And I'm saying, I simply don't think that's true. I think that for ten years, despite the official teaching of the Church, at least 85 or 90 percent of the Catholic population has been practicing birth control. It's clear that their value system is exactly the same as that of people who are not part of the Church. And this is true for members of all the mainline churches. Their values do not reflect some kind of ultra-Christian conscience. They are the values of the culture. Period! That's the way it is. The statistics say that people are not listening to the Church's hierarchy, that the hierarchy does not have effective authority — actual power — over more than a very small number of people. So to me the problem goes pretty deep. It has to do with the extent to which Christians mirror the values of the culture, for better or for worse — and in some cases it is for better. So when you ask, "Where does the Spirit of God speak?" well, if 85 percent of Catholic married couples say, this is where we really stand and this is what we believe, then the hierarchy had better listen. I'm not saying public opinion polls answer the great moral problems of the age or reveal truths of the Spirit, but I am saying we have a problem.

Roche: Of course we have. But let me make sure I'm interpreting you correctly. You were expressing surprise, were you not, that I felt the hierarchy had this major role?

Leddy: I'm saying I don't believe it really matters to the majority of Catholics *what* the hierarchy says on this and many other issues — that's a statistical fact. It does matter to some.

Roche: Perhaps, but I'm prepared to challenge you on this point. I don't think the write-off is nearly that widespread. Of course, there may be a generational factor. You are a good deal younger than I am and your perspective on this point may be different.

Leddy: Well, I'm talking about Reginald Bibby's book *Fragmented Gods,** a study of religion in Canada which details the beliefs, values and practices of Canadians, Church members and otherwise. Of course, that doesn't mean we shouldn't talk about the questions you're raising: what the official teachings of the Church are and how they are arrived at. For a committed core of Catholics, these things matter deeply. But there is a bigger...

Roche: Mary Jo, what matters, I think, is not so much the actual practice of sexuality as the points at which the Church chooses to exercise its authority. Our discussion is incomplete unless we move from birth control to abortion, to the question of the Church's capacity to teach and to infuse moral values in the society around us. The point I'm trying to make is that it's important what the hierarchy says on the question of birth control because — for the very reasons you have given — they have lost credibility with the faithful, and certainly in the outside society, because they have not clearly distinguished between birth control and abortion. When the bishops are presenting their views on abortion, as the divine teaching authority of the Church, they are speaking on a question of far greater importance. They are speaking directly to the matter of the termination of life once conceived. So they do themselves and the Church a terrible disservice by allowing it to be maintained in the public mind that their resistance to birth control and to abortion are of the same order. They have not sufficiently separated these two issues.

Leddy: I agree that credibility on the abortion question is crucial. And the combination of teaching on birth control and on abortion leaves the very clear impression that both are designed to make women bear the burden of children, period.

* Irwin, 1987.

One of the deepest reasons for the hierarchy's lack of credibility on the abortion issue isn't just the incoherence of positions; it's that the statements cost nothing. Those issuing them don't have to pay any price for them. I've often thought that if, in those statements on abortion, the bishops said, "Our rectories will be freely available to any woman who needs housing, we will bear the burden with you," then the statements would have credibility. One big problem is this gap between what is said and what is done.

The other thing I want to say, Doug, is that I think you are making too much of the notion that the bishops are the only ones who teach on these issues or present the Church's position. I have often been in the situation of presenting briefs before parliamentary commissions on abortion and peace, and nobody raises questions about credibility or says I don't have a right to speak on this.

Roche: You don't have the right to issue encyclicals.

Leddy: No, but I've got a right to do quite a bit and I'm not prepared to keep harping on what the bishops say or don't say. I think that on the issues of sexuality, birth control, abortion and gender roles, maybe the people involved are the best spokespersons. In fact, bishops need to call upon women to speak where their own voices have lost credibility.

De Roo: Well, I accept that. It comes back to the question of how decisions are reached. I don't think they can be reached in abstraction any more, by one group — under whatever authority — for all other groups. There has to be consultation and a consensus that includes a variety of gifts and insights, as well as contributions from the diverse sciences.

But Mary Jo, you really challenged me when you talked about the fact that Catholics largely follow the culture. I think there's a relationship between that and the paradigm shift I mentioned. People are moving into a different level of consciousness. We are now raising the question of how the Gospel addresses this new situation. What is the message of Jesus to this culture?

Two features of our culture present massive problems. The first is instrumental rationality, which claims the right to manipulate the world in any way we choose. The other feature is possessive individualism, which maintains that happiness comes from my having as many possessions as possible rather than from who I am as a person.

Is it the case that our culture and our consciences are being shaped by these fundamental ideas? And that they also condition our response to sexuality? In that context, I believe we must listen more carefully to some of the things that were said by Pope John Paul II speaking to the youth in Montreal in 1984. He said something which I think wasn't heard in North America, because most people don't want to hear it. It was a critique of sex as commodity. And his other comments about mutual respect between marriage partners, not using one another as objects, also received scant attention — as did the whole theme of being a responsible person and not a manipulator. I'm wondering if this whole attitude doesn't bear on the question of sexual abuse, and how people look upon other people as objects to be manipulated or used. Maybe it also relates to the breakdown of marriage, the impossible expectations that some partners place on each other, wanting their own needs met rather than reaching a mutual relationship in woundedness and self-giving.

Leddy: I think this is why we're at such a critical point twenty-five years after Vatican II. It strikes me as almost a tragic point, because I think the Pope's critique of this instrumental, technological worldview is profoundly true. But it's hard for us to recognize his critique as prophetic because he hasn't really spoken or given expression to the positive values of technology. As my father said, "Everything I do is interfering with nature." And interfering with nature isn't all bad. Much of it is very good.

In this connection, it's interesting to listen to what feminists are saying: "Persons are not objects." There is a rapid development of ethical consciousness within feminist thought, and it's really promising in terms of redefining both a personal and a social view of sexuality. Some of this new thinking will coincide with Church teachings and some of it won't. But that's where the freshness is coming from — not just from the Pope but from the whole feminist movement as well.

Roche: I'm a little nervous about somehow blaming technology for leading people to think of sex as a "commodity." I certainly share your view, Remi, that the various kinds of sexual abuse, including sexual abuse within marriage, are a terrible denial of human dignity. But how can we address these questions effectively when the persistent authoritarianism in episcopal conferences shuts off discussions of sexual questions, questions of mandatory celibacy and so on. These are further examples of the attempt to put Vatican II in parenthesis. Then I hear Mary Jo saying, well, who cares about what the...

Leddy: No, it's not me that's saying it.

Roche: No, I accept that. But I hear Mary Jo reflecting a widespread view that says, who cares what the hierarchy says? This dismissal of the hierarchy is very damaging because it's played up in the media and affects the Church's credibility. And so the desperately needed infusion of moral values into our society, which Vatican II certainly offered, is undermined by this persistent use of authority that is anti-conciliar. It's not only the abortion and birth-control issues I'm talking about; I'm thinking of the mandatory celibacy question. I want to see the Church provide a stronger, more positive reflection of the values of sexuality, and this insistence on a celibate priesthood is one of the things that stands in the way.

De Roo: I'd like to open another question which has preoccupied me for quite some time, and which I think is key to what we have been discussing. It has to do with the relationship between morality and social consciousness. It is becoming increasingly apparent to me that we cannot require that people live according to certain moral standards if we do not provide the conditions within which that sort of life is possible: where people have an opportunity to make truly moral choices. In other words, there is a relationship between oppression, injustice, sheer frustration at the lack of minimal human standards, and moral issues like abortion, conjugal violence, substance abuse and so on. We have a responsibility to provide the kind of human support structures and community that allow people to live "moral" lives. Many people who are accused of breaking one moral law or another feel they have no choice. And the irony is that the very people who are most insistent on "morality" — I'm referring to the letters on the editorial pages, particularly in the "right-wing" press — are the least interested in providing the conditions of social justice. They react very strongly against what Cardinal Bernadin called the seamless garment of morality, meaning that you can't isolate an individual issue like abortion from the larger social context. My understanding of the pastoral experience is that no woman wants an abortion as such — it's contrary to her basic life attitude. But when it's a case of economic and psychological survival for a single parent with several children, abortion appears to become a logical option.

How dare we blame the individual for a situation created by a society which is not prepared to provide the social matrix of support: the affirmation, comfort and human conditions of living that make morality possible?

Leddy: Your mention of this communal matrix introduces a different perspective, and enables me to respond to things Doug has been saying that I'm not comfortable with. He's been saying that the problem is a fear of sexuality; that may be true for your generation, but for a younger generation I don't think it is. In the broader culture there is a lot of sexual experimentation, sexual license, a very uninhibited kind of sexual life on the part of many people — young people especially. I think that if in the past, in the culture of the Church, there has been sexual repression, today there is a repression of the thirst for meaning. There is a crisis of meaning in the Church itself. Meaning is always communal. One of the problems in our culture is that marriage has been made to be the carrier of meaning — the center of life's meaning — for so many people. And marriage alone can't bear this burden. I think the loss of community has had an enormous impact, partly in the divorce of intimacy from sexuality. And I think that if there is a fear about sexuality, it is a fear of intimacy. So what we see is a kind of hedonistic sex-as-object orientation, combined with a terrible loneliness and loss of community. The old institutional structure of the Church just adds to the problem because it further isolates people from one another. It doesn't create community. It isolates clergy from each other, and from the bishop. It isolates laity and priests and religious. We can choose certain kinds of structures because we are afraid of community and intimacy, yet those are what we most need. We need them deeply. To the extent that we are in community and in real relationship with one another, and in a common framework of meaning, the questions of sexuality will find their own resolution and healing.

Roche: I want to pick up on your point about isolation, Mary Jo. There are a lot of people who are isolated today — or perhaps the word is "marginalized" — because of things relating to sexuality and marriage. There is the question of divorced persons being allowed access to communion. There are the clergy who have left the ministry and married. There are people suffering from AIDS. And there are those in gay and lesbian relationships.

Now, for me, the Council affirmed that we are all in the Church together. All kinds of people — no barriers, no discrimination — because of our common baptism. That's the principle. But in fact there *are* barriers and there *is* discrimination. Let's consider the situation of homosexuals. It's fairly well established, as I understand it, that people do not choose their sexual orientation. And therefore homosexuals ought to be treated with the respect they deserve as persons.

The Vatican Council was silent on this question. Why the Council didn't say anything, I don't know. After all, there have been homosexuals since the beginning of recorded history. Perhaps it was because there was such a focus on the recovery of the idea of marriage as a covenant relationship, and so much emphasis on parenthood and the question of contraception. Perhaps it didn't seem to be an issue then. Anyway, in latter years the Congregation for the Doctrine of the Faith attempted to deal with the issue, and while the Congregation professed a certain openness to homosexuals, its restrictive ruling that homosexuals could not meet on Church premises unless they accepted the judgment that homosexual acts were immoral was considered an indignity by homosexuals. The issue now seems to have slid off into one of those limbo territories where it's not clear to anybody

SEX THE CATHOLIC WAY ‡ 71

what the Church's real position is. So I'm left with the definite sense that homosexuals in the Church are in a position of ambiguity and marginalization, and I feel a lot of compassion for people caught in such a situation.

De Roo: I accept your comments, Doug. We need a pastoral outreach that reflects understanding and respect for all persons. This is not an area where the Scriptures really speak directly, nor do I think we can pretend that there is an absolutely clear scientific base on this question. For that reason, I think some of the official Church statements on homosexuality have claimed too much.

Leddy: At the risk of repeating myself, there is a real challenge here to traditional ideas about what is natural and what is not. Most homosexuals I know are not content with statements about being treated as equals and with respect. They want the Church to say that what they are doing is normal and natural. That's where the sticking-point really is.

Roche: We do need a theology of homosexuality. It is a human concern and it must be addressed by the Church.

Since I seem to be the one pushing difficult questions, let me come back to one I mentioned before. What about denying communion to divorced persons? How does that fit with the Council's recognition of the difficulty of making a marriage covenant, on the one hand, and its emphasis on the importance of the Eucharist, on the other?

De Roo: Let me make one or two distinctions. First of all, there is the sociological dimension of marriage, the cohabitation of two people. In other words, a lot of people are simply living together, and that's marriage at the sociological level. The juridical level is where an official person blesses or witnesses a contract between two people. But a truly sacramental marriage reaches the level of a covenant, which reflects the covenant relationship between Christ and the Church, and this mutual self-giving unto death is not something which is achieved automatically just because a marriage has taken place between two baptized Christians. These distinctions have an important bearing on questions of divorce and annulment.

Leddy: Again, my perspective would be that for a lot of people this is a non-problem. A lot of people who are divorced are simply continuing to go to church. A lot of priests have married...

Roche: Are you talking about people who have divorced and remarried?

Leddy: Yes. And priests who have now married and have not been officially laicized. They just go to church and take communion anyway. So there are now a significant number of Catholics who feel that they belong to the Church and refuse to be defined out of it. For them there's no crisis of belonging. They aren't going to be pushed around by the hierarchy...

Roche: I don't think it's good enough for people to say that they refuse to be defined out. We're talking about the integrity of the institution and the teaching authority of the Church.

Leddy: Well, let me finish. I'm simply suggesting that there's no longer a crisis of belonging. But belonging isn't quite the same as commitment, and here there may be a more serious problem.

But back to the question of credibility. We have to face the fact that, where priests have been laicized, people have asked how that can be done if they were made priests for ever. And in the same way, people who are divorced ask why they can't be remarried. A friend of mine, a divorce lawyer, could never understand the Church's view of annulments because they were based on the judgment that people had not been competent to make a decision in the first place. She felt this undercut the basis of decision-making and asked if it wouldn't be better just to say, "We made a decision and it didn't work."

De Roo: But there is a difference between the ability to make a decision and the ability in faith to enter a covenant relationship. People can make very firm decisions, and realize later that they didn't have the ability to enter into the kind of covenant relationship that is the ideal.

Leddy: Well, I think my friend was saying that the ideal can be so difficult to achieve that it undercuts the reality within which most of our decisions are made. I doubt that there is any *totally* free, mature, conscious decision.

De Roo: Your earlier point is relevant here, that marriage isolated from community can introduce unbearable burdens. So I'm not blaming individuals, but I'm looking at the social destruction of marriage that arises out of our individualism. And I don't see the point of blaming Church legislation when the problem lies in the failure of community support.

Leddy: Maybe the point that's important, Remi, is that in these last twenty-five years there has been a cataclysmic breakup of various types of commitment within the Church: in the priesthood, in religious life, in marriage. In periods of transition, I think it's inevitable that there will be a breakdown of existing commitments. But all the same, we have a pastoral concern that the people whose lives have been caught in these shake-ups should be given full support.

Roche: I haven't heard much of a response to my comment that it's not good enough for people simply to refuse to be defined out. The Church insists on the importance of the Eucharist and insists that people who are divorced should be denied the Eucharist.

Leddy: Doug, I'm not saying that's a good way for things to be. I agree that it would be much more desirable to have fewer contradictions and inconsistencies. But for a time we are going to have to live with these, with some kind of charity.

But there is another question we haven't touched on. I think Catholics are pretty tolerant of weaknesses in their Church leaders and among clergy. But on the issue of the sexual abuse of children there has been a rock-bottom visceral response. I don't think those in positions of authority realized how deeply people felt about this. They didn't see the need to take the initiative in addressing the abuse; the situation was perceived as requiring "damage control." And this has created an enormous crisis in the Church: a lack of confidence in authority, a loss of trust in clergy. Maybe something good will come out of this questioning of the basic power structures in the Church, but what a price to pay!

Roche: I wouldn't diminish any of the intensity of what Mary Jo has said. It's an absolutely shocking issue. That said, the sexual abuse of children is not confined to priests. It's found in other churches, in other professions. It's found in marriage itself. So it's really a huge societal issue; when it shows up in the Church, we are all the more scandalized because the element of trust has been so violated.

De Roo: I agree. Clerical abuse is terribly destructive. Certainly because of the breach of trust you mentioned, Doug; trust is at the core of the privileged relationship between priest and people. But more than that, because breaking that trust profoundly undermines the faith of the growing child. And because so much is at stake in that breach of trust, there is the terrible aspect of secrecy and protection of the guilty. So the Church owes a deep apology and, wherever possible, effective reparation to the victims.

The hopeful thing is that the painful revelation of the truth can become an occasion for healing. No doubt this possibility could be realized in other parts of society where the same traumas have occurred. It is fundamental to realize that innocence and guilt are not always the exclusive possession of any individuals or groups in society. As you have suggested, Doug, many terrible forms of abuse have a domestic setting. In such cases there is a similar trust but perhaps not always the spiritual dimension, the spiritual dimension which would seem to justify the highest expectations.

Leddy: Sometimes it's suggested that celibacy is a source of abuse, but I think that's a red herring. I've dealt with adults who eventually recovered memories of traumas that had occurred twenty-five or more years earlier, in a home setting with nothing to do with celibacy. It's horrendous to think that we could forget something for twenty-five or thirty years, but that shows how traumatized these kids are. You know, there is a terrible adult bias in these matters. If we could ever begin to look at these experiences from the perspective of children, from the perspective of those who are most vulnerable.

Roche: I can't leave this without saying a word of sympathy for priests, who are now being tarred with a wide brush. I can't imagine that this is helping their morale, when they are having to deal with so many of the things we've been talking about. And I have to express some compassion for the victimizers, too. What were the forces that made them victimizers? Were they themselves brutalized in their youth? How are they to deal with the consequences of their acts?

De Roo: As I have listened, I have heard resonating in my heart the words and the images and the emotions expressed by Jean Vanier and the l'Arche people. They know that intimacy and community are closely linked with the recognition of our woundedness, our need to be healed and accepted. What we need is the kind of community that, instead of placing excessive demands on people in overtaxed marriages, or people who become isolated and lonely in positions of power — this can be the case even for a parish priest — affirms us as loveable in our woundedness, in our very worst moments. Because in such a community there is the kind of meaning you were talking about, Mary Jo. In such a community we can accept one another because we share the same condition, and we can struggle together to become more human. If that model were reintroduced into the Church — more of a communion model than the isolating institutional model that separates us — we might also be modelling what could happen in married life, in social groups as well as in our relationships with one another on an individual basis.

✦ V ✦

THE HUNGER FOR
SPIRITUALITY

L eddy: In our talks so far it seems to me that we have been seesawing back and forth in considering the conservatives, who are trying to reinforce the institutional structures, and the liberal critics, who are trying to dismantle them. The trouble is that in this process the focus remains on the institution, so that even if you are attacking it, you end up inadvertently affirming it by giving it so much attention. So the danger in this whole dialectic between liberals and conservatives is that it remains on one level, the organizational level. Sometimes that's the right place for it — but surely not always.

Another thing that happens in the process of this "debate," and I think young people are telling us this, is that we lose the vibrant heart of what it's all about, the heart of the Gospel that should shine through the organization.

To give you an example, I was talking with a friend who used to be the Moderator of the United Church of Canada. He was saying that over the past couple of years the United

Church had been dealing with difficult issues, women's issues, the ordination of homosexuals and so on, and we were discussing the bitterness generated over these issues. He told me, "You know, I'm really glad we dealt with all those issues and dealt with them openly, but the Church is now exhausted as a Church community. I don't regret that we dealt with the issues, but in the process we didn't give enough time to nurturing the heart of why we were dealing with them in the first place."

I think that's the situation in our Church, too. We have been through a period of euphoria and then struggle, and we may debate whether it will last twenty-five years or seventy-five or a hundred and fifty, but we are going to be in this struggle for a long while. And the question is, in the midst of all this, can we stay in touch with the heart of what it's all about? We *must* do that, because the heart of the Church is the Gospel and that's what's needed in our culture now. Both Ron Graham's recent book, *God's Dominion*,* and Reginald Bibby's recent studies of religion in Canada speak of a tremendous spiritual thirst throughout this country. A real hunger for spirituality. I think we have to recognize that this hunger exists, and that it is not being assuaged within mainline religion. What people are seeking is a meaningful vision of life, a way of satisfying their desire to be committed.

When I talk to young people, I can see that they have a desperate desire to be committed. Like all of us, they have a desire to worship something greater than themselves. They have a need to pray. They have profound questions about death, about suffering. They want to know if there is reason to hope. Can they believe that there may be peace or that there may be justice or that there is a future to hope in? Let me give you another example. I was talking with a group of high school students about what was happening in Eastern Europe and I quoted Václav Havel, who said, "The greatest

* McClelland and Stewart, 1990.

lie of the materialistic culture is that there is nothing worth living for or dying for." And one of the kids said, "Well, you know, that's the same as here." A lie that our culture tells us is that nothing can be that important. And it seems to me that, at the root of prayer and liturgy and social action and contemplation, there is this faith that we can transcend our limited egos, that we can worship, that we can serve, that we can care for others.

From my perspective, the most critical question facing the Church is whether we can revitalize the spiritual heart of the Gospel within the Church. And by spirituality I don't mean something bodiless, something "up there" or "out there," I mean that which inspires us. That which really makes us breathe and makes us live. So I see that as a profound challenge for all of us. This is a really exciting moment — we live in a post-modern age that is looking for vision and commitment and there is a need for a new sense of mission. And by that I don't mean more imperialistic Christianity; I mean feeding the hunger of the age in a very unapologetic fashion. I'm talking about a vision of the Kingdom of Justice and the Kingdom of Peace, a vision that moves us to become contemplatives and also summons us to action.

De Roo: As I listen to you, I hear you speaking about disillusionment with modernity, with technocracy and with the consumerism that Bibby and others have commented on. Bibby talks about the merchandising of religion: there is a fierce attempt now by Madison Avenue to market new spiritualities like the New Age, new versions of consumerism and idolatry. I don't think it's going to pass the test of time. And I hear you saying that people want vision and commitment; they want to worship something greater. This brings me to a favorite thesis: that our very understanding of prayer and liturgy has to be put under a broader canopy, the canopy of the rule of

God. Retelling the Story, celebrating God's wondrous deeds in the midst of our pilgrimage as a community on its way to the Reign of God. Remembering that salvation is the gift of Christ, who confronted the destructive powers of the world. But we don't get that message across to the young people. They're looking for the message but somehow we don't get it to them.

Roche: I'm tempted to enter the discussion by reflecting on my own experience. For me, Vatican II was a wrenching experience. It was an abrupt transition in my approach to spirituality and I have to record the debt I owe to Vatican II for maturing me as a Catholic. The pre-conciliar Church seemed to stress a Jesus-and-me relationship. It was spirituality on a vertical line, buttressed by pious devotions. My mother would send me to Benediction. If you missed Sunday Mass, you might just as well go off to another planet. Weekly confession, Sunday Mass, Benediction — that was the accepted pattern. And I have to admit that, in my approaching old age, I still enjoy singing "Tantum Ergo" in Latin. (I'm one of the few who can do that!) Anyway, Vatican II exploded my mind because it showed me that a vertical line to God is insufficient spirituality in the modern world, where my "horizontal" relationship with brothers and sisters deeply affects me.

My spirituality was profoundly affected by a woman in Bangladesh when I was traveling as a journalist during those conciliar years. One day I went with a social worker to a village, doing research on development and poverty. I met a woman who had eight children. The signs of emaciation that you see in the children of Third World countries were very evident. The woman's husband was off in the fields and she invited us into her hut. I didn't really want to go in, but the social worker said yes so in we went. By the world's standards the woman had practically nothing, and in trying to decide what to talk about, I said to her, "What do you want in life?" She said, "Well, I'd like two things. I'd like enough food for my children and a place to send them to school." She reflected the needs and aspirations of countless millions of people who are deprived and dispossessed.

When the visit was over, the social worker and I got up and went back toward the highway where the car was. When we were about halfway there, I looked over my shoulder and the woman was running after us with a glass of warm palm-date juice. Warm palm-date juice is a delicacy in that part of the world. While we had been sitting talking, she had been heating the date juice on the outside fire, but in our ignorance we had been unaware of this and we had just got up and left. She caught up with us and handed me the date juice as a token or expression of what she wanted to give us, give to this strange, white, Western man who had dropped into her life for fifteen minutes and whom she would never see again. And when she gave it to me, I thought of the story in the Gospel of the widow who gave her penny, which was all she had. This woman had nothing, and yet she wanted to give me — by her standards, a fabulously rich Westerner — a "gift."

That moment sealed a bond between me and that woman forever. It's a spiritual bond — horizontal, if you like — and by extension it has helped me to develop an understanding, a relationship, with my brothers and sisters around the world, particularly those who are most dispossessed. I tell that story because it deeply affected me. I have found a spirituality expressed in the idea that life itself is a religious practice. I don't mean to say that the sacraments and the Eucharist are unimportant; I feel enriched by my involvement in the liturgy, and I am grateful to those who brought it to us in the vernacular and modernized it so that it would be more a community experience. I am one of the many who seek out a church where there is a community aspect to the Mass, as distinct from a service-station approach where you are just go to be "refueled." That being said, I approach spirituality in terms of human need in the world today, the violations of human rights that are seen most profoundly in the development and extension of nuclear weapons, in widespread poverty, in environmental destruction as well as the deliberate and specific violations of human rights. I find spirituality in living a life that reaches outside me to a hurting world.

Leddy: Thank you for telling that wonderful story, and let me try to pick up from what you were saying. You say that you came out of this vertical spirituality and that Vatican II was really a turning-point that allowed you to see that this commitment to the other was another form of transcendence. But what about young people today? They are children whose insertion into religion often takes place on the horizontal level: community relationships, service to others, things that are emphasized in the schools or wherever. They don't have the traditional sense of mystery, transcendence, awe. What needs to be reclaimed — without escaping from the world — is this sense of ultimate meaning, of something that transcends what meets the eye. And I think that unless we can put those two kinds of experience together in a new way, all we have is two fragments — which is what we often see today. You see activists who are running around like crazy, a kind of baptized version of the workaholism so prominent in our culture. The other extreme is New Age interiority, a spiritual self-development which is highly privatized and often, I think, escapist. But in each of these two there is a dimension that is authentic. These dimensions have to be brought together for a generation that hasn't grown up within a framework of symbolic meaning, with a strong sense of sacramentality. When that woman gave you the warm date juice, you were so imbued with the story of the widow in the Gospel that you immediately understood your experience in terms of that parable. Today somebody can give a visitor warm date juice and it doesn't evoke any more religious meaning than a vending machine.

Roche: I agree — I didn't mean to create the impression that activism alone is enough, nor indeed that I myself believe in a frantic activism in dealing with the social problems of the world. I do feel the need periodically to go to a monastery where I can detach myself for a few days from the relentless pressures of scheduling. In espousing a spirituality that depends heavily on "horizontal" relationships, I don't neglect the vertical dimension. It has often been said that the cross symbolizes a combination of the vertical and the horizontal. But let's go back to what you said, Mary Jo, in your opening comment — that a lot of people have this hunger for spirituality. You were also talking about people who feel there is nothing worth living or dying for in this world. In my view, those people misread the signs of the times.

When you combine Vatican II's understanding of the Church as the "People of God" with the technological fact that today we could feed every person in the world if we had the will, there is plenty worth living and dying for. There are countless examples. Think of Archbishop Romero being gunned down for his stand against repression and injustice in El Salvador, and the six Jesuits and two women who died in the same struggle. Those people saw things to live for and to die for.

Leddy: I think you misunderstood me, Doug. Václav Havel's point was that this lie, that there is nothing worth living for or dying for, is a natural extension of our materialistic consumer culture. If the self is defined by what it owns, that self will not readily be given away or given over.

Roche: But I am saying that, despite the distortions brought about by technology in our society, that same technology shows us how much there is that's worth living and dying for. We live at a time when we have an electronic bonding with people throughout the world. We understand the needs of humanity far more now. My great-grandfather came from Ireland in the middle of the potato famine. He and his brothers got on a boat — what a wrenching moment for their parents to realize they would never see these young men again! — and they came out to this strange place called Canada in search of survival. What did they know about Latin America, Asia and Africa? I mean, those places were just names. In the short span of this century, we have lifted up humanity's understanding of itself in a planetary sense. And now we have instant communication. Think of the Tienanmen massacre. We saw those faces on television day after day, and then the troops came, and the massacre. For me it was like a death in the family, because I felt I knew those people, even though they were ten thousand miles away. That's a fabulous advance in human understanding of who we are, and it speaks volumes to me about spirituality.

Leddy: What you are saying is simply wonderful. But you probably wouldn't feel that way if there weren't some very deep faith there, the kind of vision that gives you hope, a belief that we can feed the world, your own sense of power that these things can be done. But there are people in Canada right now who feel powerless to do anything about their country or about their world. What we need is a sense that there is a power operating in the world, a power that is full of promise. Without that, one can watch television, look at all those faces and go numb at the sight of all the things wrong in the world. Without a belief that God is working in the world and that we are part of God's work, there is just despair.

If it's all up to us, it can seem pretty hopeless. A really profound faith makes a very big difference.

De Roo: I'd like to pick up on the question of faith and the power of faith. I came back from the Vatican Council with my head full of all kinds of new ideas about the liturgy. I was enormously excited by all the gains we had made, and I could go on about that. But I want to speak specifically about a personal experience of discovering a deeper dimension to the liturgy, an experience that has affected me ever since.

It happened in Latin America, in a suburb of São Paolo, on a Sunday morning. I was in what we would call a priestless parish, with a group of peasants who by Western standards would be rated illiterate. Only one in the group was able to read the Scriptures. I sat there with a couple of companions and listened and prayed with these people. And what did I experience? They were linking their life stories to the great Story of salvation and redemption, although without using technical terms. All the people in that church knew they might not be alive the next Sunday. They were listening to the sole person among them who could read the lessons of the day, and in the course of the celebration they were commenting, in terms of their own lived experiences from day to day, on what those Scriptures meant to them. And they were drawing real inspiration and hope from the fact that they could remember the Story, compare their own stories and recognize that they were part of the larger Story. I heard from them, and I later heard repeated like a refrain in other places in Latin America, phrases like "We're not afraid to die." Because these people really had meaning in their lives. When they prayed and when they sang, the roof resounded with their enthusiasm. And in the gusto expressed in their voices, I discovered a dimension of liturgy that has stayed with me ever since. It's linked to the power of the Story.

I began to realize that my own story, of having visited with these people and shared a little tiny corner of their experience, had enriched me and helped me understand that I was part of this global, universal family who are all meeting on Sunday morning to remember the Story of Jesus, the dangerous memory of how Christ overcame the powers of evil. By linking their life experiences with that Story, the peasants found meaning in what they were doing, in how they were living and possibly in their dying. They were all under suspicion and therefore in danger just because they gathered for worship or carried a Bible around. They didn't fuss over whether they would live a long life or a short life, or over how their life might be terminated. Their lives were eminently meaningful.

Leddy: I would be interested in knowing from both of you how you felt about those liturgical changes at the time of Vatican II. It was an area in which change was very obvious; in fact, I think it was the first area where change was visible. What did you feel then and how do you feel in retrospect?

De Roo: Well, I had had some experience as a Catholic Action chaplain before Vatican II, relating to young people, Catholic Action or lay apostolate leaders, who were already calling for certain things that at the time were taboo — like the right to participate in proclaiming the Scriptures, the right to the cup, the right to have their opinions heard. I remember listening to one young man speak about some of these things at a Catholic Action gathering and then hearing the local bishop indicate that he didn't want that young man in his diocese again. Shortly after, Vatican II agreed with the young man's claims. So I began to appreciate the importance of such an apparently simple thing as bringing back the vernacular, because it empowered lay people, it gave worship back to them. They were no longer relegated to being passive recipients of the ministry of a priest who alone knew the Latin. Beyond that, I began to see in the revised liturgy an opportunity for a whole renewing and reactivating of our faith expression in a much more meaningful way — a linking with our real lives.

More recently, another experience I've had has been to watch the development in smaller communities without a priest, where lay people, lay leaders, have taken on the direction of the liturgy. In many situations where there is no priest to preside, alternative liturgies (or para-liturgies) have been developed. They have been used at Sunday morning celebrations, or at special gatherings, conventions or meetings. There is much more interest now on the part of lay people in the liturgy as a whole, and in developing rituals, because they have felt their life stories being linked to what they are doing on Sunday. I see lay people in the Diocese of Victoria asking for an increasing number of para-liturgies to celebrate key moments in life — rites of passage to mark important events and to bring meaning to some of their experiences at conventions or weekend gatherings, or in their families. They are looking for symbolic ways to express the meaning of what they are doing. That's been my own experience. It's really exciting to watch this renewal happening.

Roche: I'd like to come back for a moment to Mary Jo's reactions to my description of Main Street spirituality, when she said I had a faith to draw on which supported me. She described powerlessness as a characteristic of many people today. I am a bit bewildered by this depiction of powerlessness. For me, Vatican II was an empowering experience — not because it empowered Doug Roche, but because it empowered the People of God. The message of Jesus about the Reign of God, which implied so much about social justice, will find a way of surfacing as a result of what Vatican II did. This is why I don't worry too much about a lot of the things we have been pointing to here as impediments. Vatican II spirituality, the cumulative effect of Vatican II documents, moved us from being a cultic Church, separated from the world, to a Church connected with the whole human family. The world is not all white and Western — in fact, the white, Western, rich world is very much a minority in the human family — yet it is by far the most powerful part of it. And when Vatican II told us that the joys and hopes and griefs and sorrows of all human beings, especially the dispossessed, were the concern of all followers of Christ, that seemed to me to point the way toward empowerment.

Mary Jo, I reject this idea that people are powerless and that only the Secretary-General of the United Nations or the prime minister of this or that country or the Pope or an officially designated leader has power. The very dynamic of our time is that we all have an opportunity one way or another of sharing our problems and our strengths. We're not all Mother Teresas and we're not all in high office, but there are organizations galore — depending on your taste and abilities — for you to connect with on social issues and social outreach. And spirituality, I conclude, comes from reaching out and doing something for people beyond ourselves. This comes back to my point about technology — we are aided today by the very fact that we can look at a picture of the planet and see its unitary aspect, and recognize it as a marvelous creation. The woman in Bangladesh is not a stranger; she is connected to me. That's spirituality today. And anybody can have it.

Leddy: Doug, the first thing I've got to say is that you should go on the road! You've got to preach. I think you should be a priest — I think that's really what you want.

Roche: We've already discussed the impediment to my being a priest!

Leddy: You do have a message, you know. It's a message of hope: "You've got power. You can do something!" But yours is the typical confidence of people who have been in positions of power. Who know they can do something. And I would challenge you when you say that if people feel powerless, they should just somehow wake up. I think Remi has often made the point that the social context and the economic context can greatly influence people's view on life. The fact is that young people in Canada today, in the United States today, do feel powerless in the face of the big issues. In Canada we have been through the debate on free trade, the Goods and Services Tax, Meech Lake. And all sorts of people feel they fought these great battles and nothing happened, there was no change. They look at the economy and they say there are no jobs. And in the U.S., huge numbers of people don't even bother to vote. They feel completely removed from the political process.

De Roo: I want to offer something that has been running through my head. It's a proposal to rediscover the liturgy as a source of inspiration, a source of empowerment. To begin with, I suggest applying the concept of the Jewish Sabbath to our Sunday — taking a time of rest, getting away from the rat race and the daily occupations or preoccupations, to spend time in a Sabbath atmosphere. It would be centered around returning the Scriptures to the people, an idea inspired somewhat by Carlos Mesters' book, *Defenseless Flower*. The focus would not be on technical "scientific" exegesis but on reading the Scriptures in relation to people's life experiences.

First of all, as we gathered, we would come together to remember who we are, prepared to relinquish some of the dominant Western values which affect us all, conservatives as well as liberals. Then, by sharing our stories and linking them to the great Story, we would find new sources of inspiration and energy. We could take our liturgy out of the rather rigid structuring that we have tended to put around it. We could let the story of liberation, which is there in the Scriptures, speak to us. I think a lot of people, including young people, might be caught up in this and get quite enthused over participating actively in the sharing of stories in this context. That is my proposal. What do you think?

Leddy: It sounds to me as though you are building very creatively on the liturgical changes which began with Vatican II. That's very important because I think the symbolic dimension of liturgy and sacraments is valuable just in itself. I say that because people like George Grant and Herbert Marcuse tell us that technology has made our lives one-dimensional. We live our lives within a framework of scientific rationality, and it's an impoverishing experience. We need to be able to dream. We need to be able to imagine, to draw on symbols that are not just useful, not just common sense. For this reason, it is important to keep a focus on the liturgy and the sacraments. Baron von Hügel said that the greatest temptation is to follow our *idea* of Christ instead of the real Jesus. And how do we discern whether we are following Jesus in our world today or just following our idea of Christ? He said two things are important in order for a person to be connected with the real Jesus: fidelity to the Eucharist and service to the poor.

De Roo: I'm happy to hear you say that, because to me the Eucharist and the poor are not two separate thrusts but are indissolubly linked. We have forgotten that Jesus' words instituting the Eucharist, which say, "Do this," are not just an invitation to ritualize. They are a challenge to do what Jesus did, which was to offer his life for others. This is central to Christian spirituality. We have over-intellectualized the Eucharist, placed it in a very individualistic framework, and forgotten the most ancient tradition — that the Eucharist was the sharing of bread, of what we are and what we have, particularly with the poor.

✟ VI ✟

THE CRY OF THE POOR

De Roo: I want to share a short story. It's in two parts. Part one is in the year 1980, in a small village in Nicaragua. I'm sitting with eight or ten peasants in the backyard of the rectory in a little gazebo that just barely shades people from the sun. These peasants are illiterate by Western standards, but certainly not without wisdom. They have assembled in this place from Costa Rica, from Guatemala, from El Salvador. They are discussing the aftermath of the Sandinista victory, and congratulating themselves on the fact that the new government is proposing social programs for the benefit of the poor. The gist of what they are saying runs something like this: "Isn't it encouraging that this new government appears to be ready to espouse the historic cause of the poor? We hope it will remain faithful to that cause. If it doesn't, we'll find another government." These peasants wouldn't recognize the boundaries we draw on our maps of Central America; they are very conscious that they are one great people. They are aware of their place in history and they are moving forward.

Later, I talk with Jon Sobrino, the theologian, about the whole situation. He insists that the poor of Latin America, the peasants particularly, do not want revolution and bloodshed. They don't needlessly expose themselves to these bloody contests, for they are the ones who always pay the price. But when the historic moment comes, they will take one step forward and they will never go back.

Then I came home — and this is part two of my story — and I began to listen anew to the voices of the aboriginal peoples here in British Columbia. I sensed the same themes arising in their thinking and in their concerns. All this made me realize that there is an awakening consciousness of a Third World — or a Fourth World — which is revolting against the neocolonialism of today. These people are determined to empower themselves. But this historic movement is facing massive opposition from the new global division of labor. The multinationals are scheming together to take control of the economy of the world. They are promoting the globalization of capital, seeking control of the world's resources in such a way as to overpower labor and use workers for their commercial, military or political purposes.

I don't see how the Church can be neutral in a situation like this — all the more so when we think that by the year 2000, just around the corner, some 80 percent of Christians will be living in the countries we call the Third World. Our Euro-centered concept of the Church is due for a massive change, which will of necessity be intimately linked with the future of the poor.

Roche: There is so much to say in this area. I want to begin by paying tribute first of all, to you, Remi, as chief architect of the Canadian bishops' 1983 statement, "Ethical Reflections."

De Roo: One of several architects. I would not call myself the chief architect.

Roche: All right, one of the architects. There were angry attacks on that statement from many politicians, business people and editorial writers who felt the Church should stick to "spiritual" matters, but in fact the statement indicates very clearly the Canadian bishops' moral leadership on behalf of the poor, the dispossessed, those who are economically discriminated against and exploited. It reflects the teaching of the Church found in a series of papal encyclicals beginning with *Rerum Novarum*, published one hundred years ago, an encyclical which called attention to the needs of labor and whose anniversary was marked by the most recent statements of the Canadian Conference of Bishops on "The Crisis of Work" in Canada today. There have been some remarkable statements from the Vatican Council since: *Gaudium et Spes*, *Pacem in Terris*, *Populorum Progressio* and so on. So I begin by affirming the leading role that the Church has played in awakening the consciousness of the Catholic community around the world, and, in some measure, carrying into the economic and social order the values of Jesus. For me, this has been the Church at its finest. And when it comes to putting words together to form a powerful message, it would be difficult to find anything better than the words of Pope John Paul II in Edmonton when he excoriated the North for its callous treatment of the South:

> Poor people and poor nations — poor in different ways, not only lacking, but also deprived of freedom and other human rights — will sit in judgment on those people who take away these goods, amassing to themselves [the key words] the imperialistic monopoly of economic and political supremacy at the expense of others.

I've made my first point, about the leading role the Church plays through its official statements — although I must say it would be nice to hear more of this teaching echoed from the pulpit. But I have to go on to say that, while words and teaching are important, they do not seem altogether adequate, given that the forty-two least developed countries in the world, containing a population of close to a billion people, went backward in economic and social development during the 1980s. I don't think the empowerment of the poor — which you referred to, Remi, in your opening comment — is sufficient to meet the crisis emerging in the world, even when combined with the Church's moral leadership. The world is being broken up into major trading blocs of industrialized nations, which leaves the poor nations worse off than ever. And in addition to the backward pace of their development in the 1980s, these nations are undergoing a population explosion and are facing environmental destruction caused by the denuding of forests and the erosion of soil and farmlands. The result is a refugee problem now reaching massive proportions. The number of refugees doubled in the 1980s. There are now at least at least eighteen million extraterritorial refugees, with a similar number of intramural refugees in their own homelands. And to all this one has to add the effects of militarism and the arms race. The expenditures on arms by the developed nations during the Cold War was scandalous, but the expenditures on arms in Third World countries quadrupled in the 1980s. They rose at a much faster rate than even in the industrialized countries. Money was spent by governments that couldn't afford it, and their own people were deprived of their legitimate needs for human development.

But all this is a problem that goes far beyond what poor little base communities can do. I don't diminish the importance of such communities for one moment, but I recognize that the global strategies developed by the United Nations for international development must be implemented. At the very least, there must be negotiations between the North and the South for a more just distribution of the resources of the world — in the name of global security, let alone human justice.

Leddy: I don't think I can respond to either of you except to say, "Ditto." So maybe I'll start on a different tangent.

Let's again place what we are talking about within the question of Vatican II twenty-five years later. It strikes me that the mandate of Vatican II said, go into the world. Be in the world. That's where you belong. This is what you said was so liberating for you, Doug: go into the world! But I doubt that it was really until the Latin American bishops met at Medellín in 1968, and again in Puebla in 1979, that the sense of what the world was expanded to include the poor. And I think the next shift in thinking was to say that the world of the poor reveals to us what the world is really about. It reveals to us the truth of what's going on. Those two events represented very big shifts of consciousness that happened after Vatican II. Some of the poor in Latin America actually began to see themselves as part of the People of God, and at the same time it became clear to them — and to others — that the suffering of the poor was not simply an accident of history but, in large part, a product of the way the rest of the world worked.

De Roo: At this point I want to cite an extract from the Synod on Justice in Rome in 1971 — it's from Article VI of "Justice in the World." "Action on behalf of justice and participation in the transformation of the world, fully appear to us as a constitutive dimension of the preaching of the Gospel, or, in other words, of the Church's mission for the redemption of the human race and its liberation from every oppressive situation."

Leddy: So there really was a significant shift to seeing the world from the perspective of the poor. Not on the part of everyone, of course, but the shift did occur. And there was a recognition that where you live determines what you see. And I think poor people — and we need to be clear that we are talking about the poor in our own society as well as the Third World — revealed things to us that we hadn't understood. We may have known some of it theoretically but we didn't know it deep in our spirit. They made us see not so much that technology is evil but that in the hands of the powerful few it can be a tool of enormous oppression. And that the globalization of technological and economic systems made the scope of repression greater.

Here we began to see that progress was a myth of the rich; that there had been very little progress for the poor. More likely regression. So I think the poor became a revelation and provoked a shift in perspective even beyond Vatican II. There arose within the Church a sense of indignation which both of you have expressed eloquently, and that indignation indicates a deep sense that human beings are not meant to be this way. We are not slaves; we are friends of God. So the Church began to talk about the option for the poor.

De Roo: The expression "preferential option for the poor" is not explicit in Vatican II, although care, concern for the poor, was certainly there. The actual wording "preferential option for the poor" was used in 1979 in Puebla Articles 11, 34 and 35. Just for the record, that's where the phrase was coined.

Leddy: Are you sure it wasn't in informal writings and theological journals before that? I thought it was.

De Roo: I mean officially.

Leddy: Oh, officially, yes. But the "preferential option for the poor" has been a source of a great deal of dispute for some time. As you both know, the phrase has been criticized for being "exclusivist." And I personally have really struggled to understand what it means. I can't take what is said by theologians in a setting quite different from mine and simply accept it. I have to try to grapple with it myself.

It would be dangerous if we romanticized the poor in any way, and thought of them as superior moral or ethical beings. Because if they aren't — as they often aren't — then people will find a reason to write them off. That's what happened with the Israelis, the noble sabras, the minute they committed an atrocity. They were dismissed as no longer to be respected. So it seems to me very important that this phrase doesn't connote romanticism or idealization of the poor.

It also seems to me that we can't say that God loves some people more and others less. Because if God is God, each love is unique and absolute at the same time. So it has been a challenge to try to think this one through. At the same time, I know instinctively the rightness of the idea, because some of our abstract, neutral, reconciling theologies have resulted in our deciding not to take any side — which has meant taking sides with the powerful. I'd like to know what the two of you think.

De Roo: My understanding of the preferential option for the poor goes back to its roots in the Exodus story, and in the revelation of God as liberator of those who are prepared to place their total trust in God and not in the powers of nations.

You may recall how every design of Israel to become a power ended up in disaster, exile or captivity. I think what these accounts tell us is that redemption comes from God alone and that revelation only comes to those who become poor. But that doesn't necessarily mean economic poverty. We must not identify poverty as only economic, because there is also spiritual poverty. However, we mustn't escape the reality that spiritual poverty is generally accompanied by economic poverty. People who are economically powerless are often more open to hear the message of liberation.

When Jesus said, "Woe to you, the rich," he wasn't talking simply about people's money, he meant that the rich were caught by the idols of this world. They thought their human power would give them freedom and success. That's one of the constant refrains of the New Testament, and I think it explains much in the Old Testament. It does not condemn the rich as such. It simply says that to liberate or be liberated from slavery to their own riches they must enter into the experience of poverty, meaning total dependence on God. And in that sense, preferential does not mean exclusive. God's option includes everybody, but it reminds us in very stark language that the true liberation comes through the experience of poverty.

Roche: Well, if liberation only comes through the experience of poverty, I have a problem. Frankly speaking, Mary Jo, I regard the phrase "preferential option for the poor" as a slogan, and I'm not very impressed with it. We can spend a lot of time arguing these points, but I don't think they have much impact on the societal process or the political structure. I approach the problem as one who is trying to generate support among the Canadian public for stronger policies on behalf of the development process in the Third World. As a matter of fact, a substantial part of my present life is devoted to development education, so that there can be a greater understanding among Canadians of the realities of interdependence and of the North/South agenda. I'm facing headlines like "Canadians losing interest in aid to the Third World" — those words sum up several surveys which show that Canadian concern for hunger and poverty in the world is declining. And there is evidence of the same decline in the U.S.

So let's not unnecessarily complicate the already complex question of what constitutes development. I'm not saying we should identify official development assistance with the whole process of development — it's just a contribution to it. Development is what comes about as human beings are liberated economically; economic liberation is held back today by a global economic system in which there is limited access to capital and technology for the "poorer" nations. I think their cause would be greatly helped by a stronger moral voice, a stronger ecumenical voice, that would get through to the Canadian conscience.

Leddy: Well, this is why I brought the question up. I think that with believing people it's the religious imagination, nourished by the symbols and stories of the Christian tradition, that unleashes ethical action. People have to be able to imagine why this care for others, for the poor, for the globe, is a religious imperative. This is why theologians and bishops have tried to situate the issue within a religiously imaginative meaning. For instance, the image of the Kingdom of God — or the Reign of God — is very potent in liberation theology. That image stands in stark contrast to situations of oppression and poverty.

What I think the bishops and theologians are saying is that the first thing we need to do, as a religious community, is to be clear about why we have to eradicate poverty. To evoke and strengthen the "why" of this commitment to justice and peace in the world is a very important function of the Church. That is why speaking of a "preferential option for the poor" is not just jargon. It is a very deep effort to understand God's commitment to the poor, and to understand that we are committed to the poor not out of a political motivation or a psychological need — as some would say — but because this is what Jesus commanded. As I said, I have had to work out my own feelings about this, and I would put them in these terms. It is really in the covenant with the poor that the meaning of God's love is most fully revealed. These people are loved not for what they can do or what they have but just because they *are*. And I think in this particular relationship we see the absolute fullness of what God's love is about. It has to do with all of us, but the riches and wealth and greed and possessions and all kinds of things get in the way of our understanding that kind of love. And that's why I think Jesus says, "Blessed are the poor," not because it's great not to have things but because all the poor really have is God's love.

The big challenge for the middle class in North America is to see that its own religious commitments are bound up with the poor and not with the rich. The majority of our churches are middle class and many of the things we've talked about are middle-class concerns — participation, roles and so on — rather than concerns of the very poor. And yet there is a link. The link is that the poor reveal the bankruptcy of much of the socioeconomic system, and it's a bankruptcy that impoverishes the middle class as well — economically, but also spiritually. If we could become more conscious of that link, of that "solidarity," we'd have a religious imagination that could release ethical action. So to go back to the beginning: Vatican II really spoke to the middle class. Now we have another experience that the Church has said is primary, the experience of the poor, and we've got to go back to the middle class with these new insights and build not just solidarity but a kind of understanding of this historical development, which first became evident for many of us in Latin America.

Roche: It seems to me that the old business of the "comfortable pew" is getting in the way of this goal. We've got to break through the comfortable-pew syndrome, in which people basically look to the Church to support and validate their way of life. And I don't think people want to be challenged. They don't want a steady stream of challenges.

Leddy: No, they don't. But I think this culture systematically makes people passive and inactive by keeping them so busy they don't have time to think about what's going on. There are all the perks: if you just do this you'll get a television or a car; all the little numbing addictions. It's just enough to keep people hooked on the status quo. These little strings are holding everybody captive.

De Roo: I want to talk about this question of captivity. I think the rich also are enslaved. They too need liberation. The slavery to false idols can affect everybody, regardless of economic level. The moment we take a limited value like money, power, possessions, the maximization of profits, and make it a final end, then it becomes an absolute, in biblical terms an idol. It enslaves the people who worship at that altar. Preferential option for the poor does not mean not having money; it's not a thesis in favor of destitution, or returning to ancient, primal societies. It simply means that those possessions we do have, whatever their quantity, are to be used for the humanization of the world, for our sisters and brothers throughout the world. That's the crucial test. I'm not talking against development or science or progress or anything like that. It's the question of the purpose for which we use the wealth of the world.

In a certain sense, spiritual poverty consists in being sufficiently detached from the possessions that I have, whatever their quantity, that I am able to put them at the service of my sisters and brothers. This is part of what the Eucharist means. A genuine economy is the way we materially love our brothers and sisters.

Roche: It seems to me we are talking about two or three different things. We have a theological discussion of poverty and we have a rather erudite examination of what the preferential option for the poor means. And we also have urgent conditions in the world that are jeopardizing security, that are going to lead to more regional conflicts, that are going to lead to wars over resources. We have an imperative facing us, and the role of the industrialized countries in dealing with this problem has got to be strengthened.

We are facing a remarkable moment in history, when two tracks conjoin, so to speak. The first is the theological track, in which the theologians and the best of spirituality through the ages have told us that we ought to help the poor, that we have an obligation to do so. The second is a modern, pragmatic track that says that we have to repair the injustices and disparities in the world if we are to have peace and security. When you relate the disparity and dispossession to the increasing access to weapons of mass destruction, including nuclear weapons, you can see that the world is becoming exceedingly dangerous. So we have these two tracks telling us that what we have always known we ought to do, we now *must* do, if humanity is to survive. That's an imperative, that's a message the Church very much needs to get out.

But I have to say that if the Catholic Church tries to operate alone in this field, it won't be enough, and it will weaken its own position. There must be massive ecumenical programs insisting that the Canadian and American governments not slash aid in the name of reducing debt, we must make people understand that fifty billion dollars a year in interest payments is being siphoned off by the North from the South as a result of the debt crisis. The South providing money to the North is a shocking distortion of the economic system of the world. Canadians need to be told this in the strongest moral terms.

Leddy: I think we keep saying the same thing. I agree that the Church is trying to say what ought to be done. And now you are saying we must repair disparities just as reasonable human beings. A lot of people say that, but it raises once again the question of empowerment. We can recognize that we are capable of reducing those disparities, that we must do it, but the fact remains that we aren't doing it. If all people do is listen to what you are saying, you are not being pragmatic. You are not saying, now, what's the next step? My question is: will we get ourselves out of the morass that has been created by this technological, rational mindset if we remain in the same mindset?

Roche: The world's desperate people can't wait for that kind of massive adjustment.

De Roo: Doug, I want to follow up on this. There are two points I want to make. First of all, I want to go back to what you were saying about aid to the poor. I want to emphasize another dimension. It's not just assistance for the Third World that's required, it's not just charity or aid. It's an empowerment of the poor, to use Mary Jo's phrase. It's the power to bring about structural change.

Now, it's not the Church's job to define the methods for this change. But if programs to transform the world are going to be effective and meaningful in the long run, they have got to meet certain criteria. This is where theology does come in. In a situation like this, there is nothing more important, nothing more practical, than good theory. We referred earlier to the shift in thinking reflected in the 1971 synod, in the struggle between the conservative school and the reform school, and the conflictual approach that comes from the new theologies facing the question of conflict. And here is where the Church commits itself. Actually, Pope John Paul II himself, while he's cautious, is moving in that direction. On several occasions, in Latin America and elsewhere, he has exhorted the poor to be agents for social change. In his encyclical on labor, *Laborem Exercens*, he talks about solidarity with the dynamic struggle of the oppressed for justice.

Roche: You are right that aid is not enough, what counts is the empowerment of the poor. Aid is just a small fraction of the development budgets of the developing countries. What is needed is structural adjustment within many of the developing countries themselves. Such adjustment is essential for the implementation of the global strategies for development advanced by the United Nations, which focus on economic negotiations between the North and the South as to the use of resources, access to capital and relief of debt. We need a comprehensive way to relieve the Third World; we can't just muddle along on a case-by-case basis. How do you empower the poor if they cannot have health and education needs met? The first essential in the empowerment of the poor of the developing countries is that their basic needs be met: education, food, water systems, housing and so on. It's a scandal that the U.N. target — the famous target, 0.7 percent of Gross National Product — has not been met except in the rare instances of Sweden and Norway. The OECD* average is .35 percent. Canada is at .43 and is slipping. The major countries are even less. It's a scandal that what has been spent on arms is twenty-five times greater than what has been spent on development assistance. How are we going to get values straightened out in the international economic system if the religious and spiritual leaders don't give clear messages on these points? There is just too much fiddle-faddle in the churches' responses to the development crisis.

---

* Organization for Economic Cooperation and Development. Founded in 1961, the OECD includes almost all industrialized free-market nations, including Canada and the United States.

Leddy: I don't agree with that at all. That's just nonsense. In the first place, a lot of people would dispute that these things are going to be solved by increasing aid; there's no consensus on that point. I think you are looking at the question from the top down, and I think Remi and I are looking at it more from the bottom up. I don't think you can say the churches are fiddle-faddling just because they won't go along with everything you say about aid. Or that this "option for the poor" question is just flopping around.

Roche: I hope I didn't misrepresent myself as believing that aid is the solution. Structural adjustment is the solution. But the way to get structural adjustment is to empower the poor by at least helping them meet their basic needs, so they can get on their own feet. You suggest that it's not important that international aid targets have not been met and are now declining, and that Canadian interest in meeting these targets is slipping. I really dispute that.

Leddy: In some situations, one of the best things we could do would be to get out of a country.

De Roo: Get out?

Leddy: Get out of these countries and give them freedom to fashion their own economies. We bring them aid but then we proceed to impose our own values, individualism, capitalism and so on. I know situations vary, but there are real problems.

De Roo: I'd like to throw in some thoughts here, without getting into the details of the various types of aid. I think a very important thing is the model of development. And I would wholeheartedly agree with you, Mary Jo, in insisting that it's not for the First World or the Western world or the North to dictate the model of development for the peoples of the South or the Third World. It's for them to make that decision. Here is an area where we have to let go of our paternalism and our arrogance, thinking that we know what's best for everyone. It has been proven that our so-called massive aid to the Third World is effectively draining more money from the area than it's providing.

What I want to get at is how, in fact, we can support Third World liberation and development. The Canadian bishops dealt with this in a limited way in what we called, in our "Ethical Reflections" and subsequent documents, "a pastoral methodology for transforming society." We outlined five steps or phases. The first step is to identify with the poor; to be present to them, listening to their experiences. The second is to help them develop a critical analysis of the economic, political and social structures that cause human suffering. Thirdly, in solidarity with them, we must judge these situations in the light of the Gospel. Fourthly, we must help them develop creative solutions to their problems. And here I think we touch the nub of the issue: it is the poor in their own situations, the victims of various kinds of oppression, who will be able to recognize what is authentic liberation, authentic development, and what is not. This is very different from the rich or the powerful saying, we will give you money on condition that you do things according to our plan. Finally, as the poor develop alternative visions, we must, in solidarity with the victims, work toward their empowerment through a variety of networks which they can build — coalitions through which they can find the political power they need to change their society.

These five steps toward change were proposed in what was rated by some people as the most controversial section of our "Ethical Reflections." And the changes made in the societies have to meet certain criteria which were emphasized later by Pope John Paul II himself at the ecumenical service in St. Paul's in Toronto, when he practically repeated what was in the Canadian bishops' statement. To quote: "The needs of the poor must take priority over the desires of the rich; the rights of workers over the maximization of profits; the preservation of the environment over uncontrolled industrial expansion; and production to meet social needs over production for military purposes."

Those are the sort of criteria the Church can bring to bear on concrete problems. However, the ultimate judgment has to be by the poor in their own local situation. They have to determine what's best. We can't impose our models on them.

Roche: I don't think we're that far apart, Remi. Except that you have been emphasizing that we must not dictate the models of development for the poor. Of course we shouldn't dictate — but is it dictating models of development to address the urgent health, education and food needs of increasing numbers of dispossessed people? I say that they cannot be empowered, they cannot find their own route to address the systems they want to change, if they don't have a sufficient economic base for their own lives.

What I'm hearing here tonight is a certain diminishment of the aid concept. UNICEF tells us that, in the decade of the 1990s, one hundred million children under the age of five are going to die for want of sufficient nutrition, and from waterborne diseases that are easily controllable through inexpensive techniques. We urgently need to address the suffering and death resulting from the worst forms of poverty. And I'm simply saying that the people of Canada need to be galvanized, energized by the Church in this direction, for a start in the processes of development.

De Roo: I'm calling for increased aid, not diminished aid — increased aid at all levels. But the right kind of aid. Not only economic but also technological, because maybe information is the most important aid. Aid that is given in partnership and solidarity, in collaboration with the poor, aid that enables them to educate themselves and to make key decisions. Allowing them to make their own mistakes rather than making them ever more dependent in the process of helping them.

That is the critical point. Merely giving aid according to our models, under our conditions or according to our analysis of their society, makes people perpetually dependent. And I think we have a syndrome here, which we find not only at the level of government but also at the welfare level. Look at the Department of Indian Affairs here in Canada, where there is a professionalization of charity. People get their incomes and their jobs from helping other people. Then, to maintain their power, their positions, salaries, prestige or whatever, they have to keep the poor dependent. To me that becomes a very destructive form of aid. Our real goal is to help the poor empower themselves.

✠ VII ✠

WAR AND PEACE TODAY: NO MIDDLE GROUND

*R*oche: I begin with the famous quotation from one of the principal documents of Vatican II, "The Church in the Modern World," which was the only time Vatican II issued an actual condemnation. It goes as follows: "Any act of war aimed indiscriminately at the destruction of entire cities or of extensive areas along with their population is a crime against God and man himself. It merits unequivocal and unhesitating condemnation."*

Well, the Vatican Council, having condemned the use of weapons of mass destruction, advanced moral teaching on war. It went beyond the traditional concept of a just war, in which limitation and proportionality were the criteria by which a war could be judged. It recognized that we are now in the nuclear era, with its weapons of mass destruction — the smallest nuclear device today is eight times more powerful than the bomb that destroyed Hiroshima, and the existing fifty-two thousand nuclear weapons have a destructive capacity one and

---

* *Guadium et Spes*, chapter V.

a half million times the power of the Hiroshima bomb. As we go into the third generation of nuclear weapons, we see that the modernization of these weapons is continuing, and threatens our whole planet, through what scientific studies describe as "nuclear winter." Moreover, nuclear weapons are spreading around the world. There are now twenty-six Third World countries that have acquired ballistic missile technology, and six of these already have nuclear weapons. The two superpowers, having built an arsenal of some 97 percent of those fifty-two thousand nuclear weapons, have a prime responsibility to come down from the nuclear mountain that has been created.

The Vatican Council, however, gave grudging acceptance to nuclear deterrence, saying it offered peace of a sort. In other words, the Council, having condemned war, did not condemn the possession of nuclear weapons. In fact, it was Pope John Paul II who in 1982, in his address to the Second Special Session on Disarmament at the United Nations, gave what has turned out to be the definitive position of the Catholic Church today, which was picked up by the American bishops in their 1983 statement and reaffirmed in their five-year evaluation in 1988. Those views were more or less seconded by the Canadian bishops. I quote the Pope's words: "In current conditions, deterrence based on balance certainly not as an end in itself but a step on the way to a progressive disarmament may still be judged morally acceptable. Nonetheless in order to ensure peace, it is indispensable not to be satisfied with the minimum which is always susceptible to the real danger of explosion." In other words, to be morally acceptable, the strategy of nuclear deterrence must lead to disarmament. It cannot be a permanent policy. Yet, despite the end of the Cold War, that is exactly what it is.

The Church, I believe, is in a good position to put forward a review or revision of its admissibility of nuclear weapons in light of the end of the Cold War. This development in history offers us a moment for review, and certainly the Catholic Church has an obligation as a paramount moral influence in the world. It is clear that the Reagan administration was very worried that the American bishops would, in their 1983 statement, come out against nuclear weapons and challenge the validity of the nuclear weapons strategy; this would have compounded the U.S. government's difficulty in proceeding with the deployment of cruise and Pershing missiles in Europe. It is a fact that the moral influence of religion in this area is still very strong.

De Roo: I marvel at your complete possession of this subject. Obviously your career in the field of peace and international diplomacy has made you an outstanding authority in that field. I agree wholeheartedly that the churches should now unequivocally condemn not only nuclear weapons but all mass destruction weapons, including chemical and germ. I offer the following reason — with full awareness of the complexity of this situation.

Our moral decisions are qualified and conditioned not only by eternal verities or criteria or principles, but also by our experience or knowledge of reality. Our knowledge of reality has altered dramatically since the Council. For instance, because of what we have learned from the sciences, we are now aware that, as human beings, we are an integral part of our environment. As a result, our very survival is conditioned by the biological sphere. Consequently, it has become clear that any use of mass destruction weapons is a crime against humanity. I would rewrite the Vatican text in light of this present knowledge.

Now, when the Church reluctantly recognized the possibility of deterrence through nuclear arms, there were also conditions placed, which at that time we still thought were realistic. For instance, it was specified that under no circumstances should population areas ever be targeted. But today it is evident that that condition will never be realized. Not only are civilians at risk when military targets are attacked, but the whole fabric of a society can be shredded as a result of a military conflict. We simply can't be limited and localized. Consequently I would say that we must now unconditionally condemn any use or even possession of mass destruction weapons, of whatever kind, as not only unrealistic, as they will *not* bring peace, but a crime against humanity. The possession of nuclear arms eventually means their use. We have to stop waffling on this issue.

Leddy: Maybe we should speak about the context in which the Vatican II teaching on war and peace was situated. It seems to me that it took place in the shadow of the Cuban missile crisis. I think the biggest crisis since then was in the early eighties, the Reagan showdown with the Soviets. So there have been moments of crisis and then moments when the issue of war was on the back burner.

Each of you in your own way has had a lot to do with the Church's teaching on war and peace. I'm very proud of those statements and teachings; there has been a kind of consistency on this issue, and a more radical stance. I also take great pride in the Vatican statements which have consistently condemned nuclear weapons, not just for what they threaten, but because they are a siphoning-off of all kinds of money from the poor of the world. I agree with both of you that the matter of nuclear deterrence has to be addressed. The time of waffling is over. The whole concept is now just ridiculous.

However, I am concerned that the clarity of these moral statements has not been persuasive. These statements are like many other Church statements — they are general. They are strong, but the Church hasn't paid any great price for them. I don't want to call them cheap, but people do say words are easy. I think what is urgently needed is not only a statement but also a profound commitment to action on the part of the Church. I think people would really hear these things if, for example, the Church said, "Ten percent of any money we receive from our congregations will go toward peacemaking. We will hire peace officers in our dioceses, we will have a peace program, we will declare the dioceses nuclear-free zones, we will support anybody who transfers out of a job in the arms industry." This kind of commitment, not only on this issue but on other issues, would really say something. I also think that in addition to the question of deterrence, the theology of the "just war" needs to be addressed. Given the weapons of mass destruction, I don't think any circumstance would justify war any more.

I have found the last year very sobering in terms of the question of war and peace. Six months ago the wall was coming down and peace was breaking out everywhere. And then, another war broke out. To me, all of this illustrates the depth of what we are up against. It's not enough just to get rid of certain types of weapons. The military-industrial complex is like a monster with many heads. As soon as one conflict is over, it generates another. This monster feeds on war. It also, like the god Moloch of the ancient Ammonites, feeds on children. Even if its weapons are never used, they have already consumed the food and health of millions of children.

There is no escaping the challenge posed by this situation. It's not just a political challenge, it's also a spiritual one — having to do with will and desire. Until peace becomes a passion in our hearts and souls, we will not make the changes in our patterns of life that would ensure a more enduring peace. We may not be comfortable with all the military interventions taken by the American empire, but we are still too comfortable with the benefits that arise from being a dominant power in the world. Such dominance, of course, will not last forever. America is an empire in decline — at least economically.

That's what makes it so dependent on military might to assert its power. That's what makes it so dangerous.

I don't see how we can avoid asking ourselves the question: am I a citizen of this empire or one who longs for the Reign of God? Am I propping up the empire or helping to build the Kingdom? None of our actions is neutral in this regard. My concern is that we may soon lack the spiritual energy even to ask this question. The twentieth century has dished out such massive doses of human destruction that we have become psychically and spiritually numb. We are no longer shocked by "little wars" such as those in Central America, and we are incapable of being shocked by the possibility of a world war.

We need to be shaken out of this numbness. However, I don't think we'll be shaken by more fear of war. We'll be shaken, I believe, because of our love for the world and for other human beings.

De Roo: In response to your earlier point, I want to recall a basic principle for which the Church is indebted to Ignatius Loyola, a layman. Ignatius taught that we can make no proper spiritual discernment when we are not ourselves, individually and as a community, at peace. So decisions made in moments of crisis — and you mentioned that Vatican II took place in the shadow of the Cuban missile crisis — have to be re-examined in a moment of quiet to see if we are responding fully to the Spirit. I think Vatican II was responding to the Spirit in its strong reaction against war, and would have gone further if it had been able to discern more peacefully.

I would like to see all the world leaders again meet in prayer with the Pope, as happened at Assisi in October 1986, and there, in a prayerful context of retreat, make a statement about war, and be prepared to share that with the whole world as a common message. Personally, I commit myself to work through organizations of which I am a member, like the World Conference on Religion and Peace, and Pax Christi, that already have considerable influence, to help bring this about. Having clarified what religion today must really say, on the basis of our present knowledge of the fragility of our globe, our ecosystem and even the very cosmos, all religious bodies should commit themselves to specific actions like, for instance, setting aside some of their resources for a peace fund, setting up an education program, training people for peace.

Leddy: It takes something like that. If it's only words, they're a dime a dozen. I know — I'm a wordsmith. There has to be commitment.

Roche: I was quite moved by Mary Jo's statement about the events of the past year. The word that in my view describes this year is "veneer." Peace viewed in terms of the end of the Cold War is a veneer because underneath is a deeply rooted system of militarism that still dominates the world of political structures. Of course, in the Gulf crisis, the immediate deployment of massive forces of troops under the driving determination of the United States revealed all too horribly the continuing dependence on militarism as a solution to problems that are far deeper than they appear on the surface.

Talking of the Gulf crisis, I of course condemn the invasion of Kuwait by Iraq, and I offer no defense for Saddam Hussein. That said, the interconnected problems in the Middle East need to be dealt with by the whole community. Fortunately we have a world community, in the United Nations, but international institutions still need strengthening, and a process of international law that will be respected by the major powers — as well as the minor powers — still has to be advanced. It was the quick recourse to militarism in the Gulf crisis that I found traumatic, when, with the end of the Cold War, I had been expecting that we would be able to move into a period when my voice, among others, would begin to be heard. I don't think the political establishment is hearing me when I call for a peace dividend in which we begin to shift a portion, at least a portion, of the trillion dollars going into armaments around the world into economic and social development.

Leddy: I recall a conversation with Daniel Berrigan, a longtime peace activist, at the time when peace was supposedly breaking out all over. He said, "This thing, the monster of war, isn't dead at all. It's going to reappear." And of course it did reappear, because the end of the Cold War didn't arise out of any profound conversion to the ways of peace. The Soviets ended the Cold War because it wasn't making economic sense. But war as a way of life has become deeply engrained in the American empire. An enemy is needed to justify the massive expenditures on defense. The military-industrial complex was only temporarily shaken by the promise of cuts in the wake of Gorbachev's peace initiatives. Soon a new enemy was found — Noriega and then Hussein. And there will be more enemies, and ever greater military expenditures, until we are truly convinced that peace is the better way, the only way.

Roche: Peace will continue to be a veneer until we root out the militarism that dominates the political order today. I'd like to turn now to a very specific instance in which moral leadership is needed, that is, the testing of nuclear weapons.

The story of the arms race of the past four and a half decades is told in the 1,910 nuclear tests that have been conducted, 929 by the United States and 715 by the Soviet Union, the remainder by the United Kingdom, France and

China. New technologies continue to fuel the arms race. As long as nuclear testing goes on, we are going to have a continuation of the development of nuclear weapons, not only among the five major nations that have them now, but also among the increasing number of nations who are going to refuse to go into the next century as second-class members of this, the supposed new world order.

The fact that the United States has resolutely refused to stop underground testing — even though the Soviets have said they are prepared to stop on a reciprocal basis — has guaranteed the continuation of the arms race. There is the further fact that the U.S. resisted the Partial Test Ban Treaty amendment conference which took place in New York in January 1991. The U.S. rebuffed an overwhelming number of nations who wanted to convert the Partial Test Ban Treaty against atmospheric testing into a complete treaty to ban all testing. The fact that the U.S., supported by Canada, blocked that move is nothing short of a disgrace, given the end of the Cold War. The time has come for the highest leadership of the Catholic Church to speak definitively in opposition to continued nuclear testing, as the heart of the nuclear weapons question, which is at the heart of the arms question, which has a direct impact on the economic and social development of peoples around the world. The time is now here.

De Roo: I can only agree. But I want to go back to your question, Mary Jo, and I hope I'm not misinterpreting it. Is the American empire the "beast"? And are we ourselves part of that empire?

Let me illustrate what I'm getting at. We are all beneficiaries of modern technology. As much as anybody else, I'm an accomplice of the technological worldview. It's in my pores. I've been conditioned. We know from psychologists and other social scientists that it's very difficult to be critical of one's own perception of reality, because it's too threatening. Very few people have the gift of being able to step out of their own environment in such a way that they can look critically, in true spiritual assessment, at their own reality.

The American dream is in all of us. Look what happened when the Berlin Wall fell. One young activist from East Germany who had helped make that possible looked sadly at people rushing across the border to shop. "I thought freedom was about more than shopping," she said.

I understand that many of our young people today say their favorite pastime is shopping. What better illustration that we are all part of this dream? We're all accomplices, okay? Particularly when the worldview is couched in words like "democracy" and "freedom." Well, freedom is often misunderstood as the right to impose our own will.

We have centered our whole world on a concept of humans imposing their will on the world of nature, humans as masters of the world. We have even interpreted Genesis in that context, instead of recognizing the world as mystery, as part of a cosmos emerging from the womb of God. A world to be respected and revered, treated symbolically and religiously, rather than manipulated or even destroyed. We have accepted a vision of a homocentric world, with humanity at the center. We claim to be the bosses: we will dominate, we will control. But that vision is collapsing, and we are in grave danger now if we don't realize that it's collapsing, because it's clear that we could now destroy ourselves. And the cosmos, made for God's glory, could continue to evolve as if human experience, this little glitch in cosmic history, had never existed. I don't know if we realize how fragile we are. It's in that context that I said earlier that war has to be condemned absolutely. It solves nothing.

Leddy: We must find reason to hope, because this is such a massive problem. I sense that we are at a different point now than we were at in the early eighties. There was a peace movement then, but in many ways it was a kneejerk reaction out of terror. I sense now that there is much more of a rootedness on the part of a growing number of people. It's not just that they are against war; they are for a planet that is safe and ecologically balanced. It's a much wider consciousness. With the war in the Gulf, the peace movement mobilized far faster than it ever did around Vietnam — because, I think, the roots have gone deeper.

An issue I see for the future is that people are identifying themselves more as citizens of a planet than as citizens of a nation, but there is also a growing individualism. I think human beings need intermediary points of identification or association, such as church, religion or city. We cannot just live with some sense of being inhabitants of a planet. It's too vague, and often it results in people retreating to tiny, private worlds of meaning. So we have to search for those intermediary forms of commitment and association, one of which may or may not be the nation.

Roche: Vague? It isn't vague any more. Remi, of course it's important for the religions of the world to speak together, and the experience of Assisi — as what one might call a trial run — was important. That being said, the role of the Catholic Church in this set of equations, religious equations, is of first-rank importance in the world.

Leddy: Okay, you want the Church to have a strong voice, a clear voice, an international voice. But this is precisely the argument the conservatives give as to why Rome must be the voice for the Church and it must be a unified, uniform voice. They use precisely that argument against diversity, against different voices coming from the national churches.

Roche: I think, before we go much further, we have got to deal with this word "diversity." I want a universal authority to prohibit war, a universal authority to be a centerpiece of international law in protecting human rights in their multiple dimensions. That would not lead to a homogeneous state in which we all give up our cultures and religions and races. Quite the reverse — it would make the world safe in this new technological era in which we are now so vulnerable. It would make the world safe for diversity, because people would have to come to a new understanding of cooperation.

Leddy: You're not dealing with my point.

Roche: Well, look, there are always going to be arguments about diversity versus unity, but we can't be muted by our fear of giving the conservatives an arguing point. But maybe I'm misunderstanding what you're saying.

Leddy: This isn't an argument, but I'm trying to bring out what I think is central to this discussion. Your plea, which I agree with, is that the Church present clear and ethical leadership. By the Church you mean the hierarchy, Rome, the Pope, basically....

Roche: Because they are the only people the media pay any attention to.

Leddy: Now, what you are looking for is exactly what the conservatives are looking for: that in this world of chaos, in this world of moral flux and flip-flop, there must be a strong voice, a central voice, and it must be the Pope's. Conservatives want exactly the same thing.

Roche: Well, what's wrong with that?

Leddy: But you can't have it both ways. You can't say you love it when the Pope speaks with this clear voice on peace but you really don't like it when he says, "My dear brothers and sisters, in this time of moral chaos the celibate priesthood is God's will." I'm just playing devil's advocate, but I...

Roche: This is very interesting. I'm hearing you, but if you want to talk about celibacy and world peace in the same sentence, you'll have to find another partner to talk to. I can't put them in the same sentence. For me the obliteration, the threatened obliteration, of life on this planet, which is the immediate subject here — our concern about the immensity of nuclear weapons — is of such magnitude that it cries out in the name of God for moral leadership. This must supersede all these itsy-bitsy problems we have inside the Church. And I say, let's have more of the Pope and his fellow religious leaders of all faiths, via Assisi, via the World Conference on Religion and Peace, via a serious interfaith effort, to awaken the conscience of humankind and force the political system to respond to the new reality.

Leddy: I think you are reinforcing the power of Rome. You've done that all along. What I feel is that popes have spoken strongly against war for twenty-five years and it hasn't been heard.

Roche: But what would you have: a jumble of voices? Everybody doing their own thing? The people, the media, regard the Church as an institution, as an "entity," as a juridical force, and in the pragmatic terms in which you and I operate, it's the only thing the media pays any attention to. If we are going to get through via the media, to influence public opinion, it's got to be with a voice that is recognizable and identifiable.

Leddy: I don't agree.

Roche: They ought to listen to Mary Jo Leddy, and they ought to listen to me. The fact is, they don't listen to us. But they are all ears for whatever the Pope says.

Leddy: Are they? People say the papal position against war is the best-kept secret in the Catholic Church. I can tell you a funny story, because the bishop involved is dead. I had a phone call a couple of years ago from two women in Vancouver. They asked me to come out and speak at the spring peace walk and I said, well, get somebody from Vancouver and save yourself some money. But they said, the archbishop here is against all this peace stuff and the priests are too afraid to speak, so it has to be somebody from outside. So they hauled me in and for three days I was on prime-time talk shows, and I cited every papal encyclical I could, indicating what the Pope had said about peace. By the end of the three days, there was little doubt that the Church was for peace. But that was news to people. Most people didn't know it. And that's not just the case in Vancouver. It's a total secret. The cognoscenti know what's in these documents but it's not popular teaching. Everybody knows what the Church teaches about contraception and birth control but they don't know what the Church teaches about peace.

De Roo: I think you have made your point very clear. As I listened to you, I picked up a couple of things that I want to come back to, by way of bringing this to the local level.

When I arrived in Victoria, there was practically no relationship between the Church and the University of Victoria, which was founded in 1964. Since then, things have evolved. I'll spare you the details, but recently I made a proposal to the university for the setting up of a center for interdisciplinary dialogue between the sciences and the religions of the world. That's now moving through the regular academic decision-making processes.* I hope the center will be a setting where there can be discussion around those fundamental concepts of what constitutes the human, and what the basic needs are for the survival of our civilization. Discussion could take place between representatives of the major religions and the various sciences, on values, on matters spiritual as well as pragmatic. Increasingly, science is realizing that there have to be some values, some ethical directions, that are mutually acceptable. This is a concrete example of the kind of thing that can be happening at the local level. Here would be a forum — watch out, you two, you may be invited to speak! — a platform to bring this information not only to Catholics, but to all the people of the area.

Roche: I'd like to make a comment about peace that I think is important and appropriate in this discussion. What is peace? My political and diplomatic experience has convinced me that peace must begin in our hearts, that there is a very strong ethical dimension, a moral, spiritual value, that not only should not be lost, but should be reinforced. This is precisely why, Mary Jo, the Church in its pastoral life should be energizing people with this reality. The Gospel tells us very clearly that we must be reconciled with one another in the world, and the older I get, the more I realize how important that quality of reconciliation is, whether it's in terms of our own family, our associates and colleagues or the world order.

That's why it's a beautiful experience to see the reconciliation now occurring between people who lived under Communist systems and people of the West. The commonness of our humanity is now celebrated, and where this must begin is in our own hearts. Without hesitation, I can say that this is what my own work is about, trying to advance issues of peace. That is the centerpiece of my own life, my own professional life. I feel that if I am to espouse peace, I must feel peace in

* The University of Victoria has now approved the establishment of the center.

my own heart and with those around me. This is where I begin, and my work at the international level is simply an extension of that process.

De Roo: I want to pick up on that, Doug, and apply it to the apparent failure of ecumenism to date. I think you are right on target. One of the main reasons why so little has happened for peace is that the churches themselves have not yet been reconciled. This is because of a shallow ecumenism that is more preoccupied with safeguards, with congregational promotion, the recruitment of members, than with real evangelization in the cause of the Prince of Peace. Instead of promoting the Reign of God and committing ourselves to bringing about the peace announced to the world at Christmas, we have been into the "numbers" game. This morning I was at prayer, reflecting on today's readings as I prepared for this discussion. Luke 4 tells of Jesus entering the synagogue at Capernaum and reading Isaiah's prophecy about the "year of the Lord." He makes a proclamation that this prophecy has now been realized. The people marvel at the "words of grace" that flow from his lips. The Prince of Peace has come. I was also reading first John, chapter 4, where he says, "Unless we love our brothers and sisters, we are liars if we say that we love God."

Now, to me, loving our brothers and sisters involves economics. Because sharing our wealth is how we love, practically speaking and in the context of the questions we have been discussing. The Eucharist also has meaning in terms of economics, not to mention politics. To be faithful to our call to Eucharist, our call to conversion and our call to ecumenism, we have to link peace with global economics, and with the kind of development that is just. That calls for a conversion of attitude, and a conversion of attitude is only the beginning. I think we need to call our congregations — and I am committing myself to work on this — to begin to be reconciled locally. Perhaps this can be part of our Mission for Peace for the year 2000, to bring about this reconciliation at the local level. Each one of us can start doing something in a very concrete way. By symbolic gesture, action and commitment, we begin these reconciliations at the local level, without which there will never be worldwide reconciliation — notwithstanding all the beautiful theory and all the declarations that are presently being made.

Leddy: I think what the two of you are saying is very profound. It's a real conundrum I've experienced in terms of pastoral work and also political work: what, really, does peace mean? It's so easy for people to think peace is a kind of psychological feeling of tranquility. Some of the New Age stuff affirms this kind of peace. But I think interior peace has more to do with a sense of rightness. A sense of rightness, not a feeling of tranquility, which can often be false — especially in what have been called addictive systems, systems that foster a denial of reality, that strive for peace at any price. In systems like that, peace is seen as the obliteration of all opposing positions, the obliteration of tension and division. And that kind of peace or reconciliation can become an ideology to crush internal conflict and dispute.

De Roo: The peace of cheap grace.

Leddy: Exactly. Politically, it's the peace of the dead: you will finally have peace if you just kill off enough people. So it's difficult to present an image of peace that is really authentic, that includes justice, that includes truth and conflict, as part of the process of achieving peace.

Roche: Just a minute. Both of you have evoked in me a deep-seated fear that only my faith enables me to overcome. It's this. Throughout the history of the human journey, there has been conflict, which has led to aggression and wars and so on. What has produced it? One might say greed. One might even say the simple condition of humanity. In our own tradition, we might say that it's the consequence of original sin. Does that mean it's beyond our possibility to live in harmony? We have come out of the caves and now reached the point of nuclear development. It's a real question to me whether the human family is capable of peace. What *is* clear is that the technological advance of weaponry has brought us to a stage where, in the interests of our mutual survival, we must outlaw war. So from the pragmatic point of view, war is obsolete, and the best I feel I can do, as a politician-type person, is to reinforce the idea that we can no longer resolve conflict by war because of its massively destructive dimensions. As for the resolution of conflict as such, that would, of course, be a big step forward for humanity. To outlaw war might give us a chance, in what Remi calls a cooler atmosphere, to identify the deeper sources of conflict.

What is peace? Peace is a lot of things. I'll settle for "peace as development," and I thank Paul VI for that phrase, because it gives you something to work with. If you understand peace as development, you see how we must reach out to our brothers and sisters around the world, to make their human lives livable.

De Roo: If we really look at war in any form, nuclear, Cold War or whatever, we see that one of its consequences is the transfer of wealth to the global transnational corporations, under the guise of patriotism. As a result, the working class, all the working people of the world, are called to collaborate in the further globalization of capital and increased international debt bondage, as all these little nations rush to arm themselves to the teeth with arms that everybody hopes they will never use. And to pay for all that, they virtually starve their own populations. Arms now become a means to enforce the International Monetary Fund and World Bank policies, to ensure that development conforms to the Western model. This means resource-export economics, crops produced for export, enriching a small number of wealthy capitalists and taking food out of the mouths of peasants. No wonder regional conflicts keep popping up all over the world! We may end up locked into a war economy in the name of development as peace.

Leddy: I don't have a whole lot more to say. I think it's one thing to say that war is obsolete. But we could leap from there and say that conflict is obsolete — and I don't think we should say that. I think we should say that not only will conflict always be with us, but it *should* be with us, because wherever there are differences there will be conflict. All too often the Church has dealt with conflict terribly. Conflict with other religions has all been in the name of unity and truth, and it has been terrible. The best example of dealing with conflict was in the medieval universities: two sides debated, not necessarily agreeing. There was within those medieval universities a free space in which conflicting opinions and views interacted, with no effort to resolve them totally. What went on was a kind of mutual corrective that enhanced the search for truth. So I think we have a challenge as to how to welcome conflict as creative, and as leading to truth, in a way that is not destructive of persons or whatever. And that is a big challenge.

De Roo: This is a very different approach to wisdom from the so-called scientific approach today, which tends to reductionism, to looking at things from one angle instead of several aspects. When science was still in a primitive state, this is what the Scriptures said: "Hear what wise people say." The wise look at all sides, all different perspectives. And this leads me to a further point. As I look at the developing teaching of the encyclicals, of the teaching authority, the Magisterium, at various levels, I do see a sign of hope. I see a definite line of growth in better identifying the problems of underdevelopment, the problems of militarism and the ways to deal with them.

Roche: I am still left with a question about the Church's role in enriching our spirituality, in firing our hearts so that we can reach out to everyone, in different parts of the planet. At the practical level, of course, certain structures and instruments are required. We have to replace war with other forms of conflict resolution. We have to develop further our peace-keeping forces. We have to strengthen international institutions like the U.N. Security Council. There has to be a whole body of international law by which we can manage the planet. But I want to pick up on what Remi was saying about the role of the Vatican....

Leddy: Are you still looking to the Vatican?

Roche: The reason Vatican policy or spokespersons for Vatican policy are so important is because of a simple reality. The Holy See is a state which occupies a seat as an observer at the United Nations. It doesn't vote but it certainly has a role in a consultative capacity. And the presence of Paul VI and John Paul II, in person, at the United Nations was a profoundly important political event. They had an impact by virtue of the position occupied by the Holy See in world affairs. This is why the foreign policy of the Vatican is a very practical question for us to consider as we look at post-conciliar Catholicism, in terms of peace. Several times in this dialogue, we have referred to *Pacem in Terris* as a seminal document, espousing human rights. That was followed by Pope John's opening to the East, at a time when it was considered bold, if not foolhardy, to have any truck or trade with Communism. When Pope John Paul II received Gorbachev on the steps of the Vatican, so to speak, that was not only a turning-point in relations between Christianity and Communism but an example of that process of reconciliation which I have been saying is crucial for the achievement of peace in the world. These forward steps in Vatican foreign policy have an impact on the world and they must not only be continued and encouraged, they must also be reflected at the local pastoral level.

De Roo: And that was what I, too, suggested earlier. At the deepest level, peace is something profoundly spiritual. But its meaning is worked out in our relations with each other, one to one, in our communities and in the economic and political and cultural spheres across the whole planet. It is not just one of these things taken in isolation. It's all of them together.

POSTSCRIPT*

Roche: As I think back on the Gulf War, there are three reflections I would like to offer.

First, we have learned that war, not peace, is the dominant energizer in our society. The speed of the military buildup in the Gulf, the quick recourse to war, the dominance of the military in political thinking and in manipulation of the U.N., the public cheering of the highly technological warfare by the most technologically advanced powers and the postwar determination to increase the arms trade — all of these indicate that war, not peace, is what drives our society. I had previously thought that the end of the Cold War might galvanize a new social direction toward peace. That didn't happen.

* The following was recorded during a telephone conference call early in May 1991 (see introduction).

The second lesson is that we now know we have an immense ethical problem in addressing the question of respect for human life. We now know that the political order is not capable of responding to human needs. The sluggish response to the exodus of the Kurdish refugees, in contrast to the striking swiftness of the prosecution of the war, reveals the bankruptcy of political concern for the most dispossessed people of the world.

Finally, it is now clear that we need an extraordinary campaign to support the morality of life in what is described as the "new world order" beginning to unfold. What is desperately needed — and the Gulf War and its aftermath clearly point this up — is a massive push for a moral base for life on this planet.

De Roo: In my view, what has happened is that a superpower, because of its technological advantage, has in effect been able to say to the Third World, "Don't get in our way because we will do whatever we need to do to protect our interests." I would like to identify two economic factors which led to the war: the need to guarantee access to oil and the lucrative profits — in many quarters — from arms sales. The lesson to the smaller powers is that they will simply have to knuckle under to whatever the reigning superpower or superpowers wish to impose.

My next point is somewhat similar to yours, Doug. I'm very much concerned about the possibility of continuing serious moral discourse in the euphoria which has followed a quick and supposedly clean war. I say supposedly because during and immediately after the war, we had documentation mainly from one side. We didn't hear a lot about the terrible destruction of human life. The world was given a one-sided picture and all attempts at genuine moral discourse seemed to be drowned by a flood of military propaganda.

The classic conditions for a just war are well known, but they do not appear to me to have been fulfilled in this case. Were the intentions right and were the actual objectives made clear? Was there, in effect, a just cause? Was waging the war really a last resort, considering that the embargo had been given such a short time to succeed? Was there proportionality between the damage done and the positive results achieved? These considerations were never given a full debate. So I would join you in saying that there is a tremendous challenge now to all people who really believe that respect for other human beings is basic. There is an urgent need for a deepened moral discourse in the world to achieve harmonious relationships based on justice, not force. There is a need to rebuild a moral climate and to affirm universal principles and values on which a just world order can be constructed. We need more than political solutions. There is a fundamental ethical issue facing us.

Leddy: The war for me was a traumatic event. It calls for a very serious reassessment of our situation as a Church. In many ways, what happened simply deepened my conviction that we are living in a profoundly destructive empire and that we are operating, by and large, out of a Nintendo morality. We are bombarded by propaganda, information is censored, and I think it is very questionable whether we can call ourselves a democracy in the deepest sense of the word. Another thing that disturbs me is the obvious fact that churches and religious leaders exercised almost no influence in this situation. Church leaders spoke strongly at all levels but it made absolutely no difference. They were just voices in the wind.

According to the latest Gallup poll in the U.S., 90 percent of Americans are affiliated religiously, predominantly as Christians, and 90 percent of Americans supported Bush in the Gulf War. In Canada the support was very similar, since we are essentially a colony of the American Empire. It seems to me that the apparent weakness of the churches' moral suasion should make us think. Either we ignore the situation and play "Let's pretend," or we go one of two ways. We can see the Church as a very small corner of society which can assume the sort of position the Mennonites have always had as a minority "culture." Or we can see a task of evangelization in a pagan culture in front of us — we can see ourselves called to a new mission, a moral mission. Either case would call for a profound conversion on our part.

Roche: Mary Jo, you said that the voices of the churches were like voices in the wind and that they had no effect on the political decisions at the time of the war. I agree with that, but there was not a clear religious opposition to this war, just as there is not a clear religious opposition to the strategy of nuclear deterrence. There was not a clear message on the Gulf War. The mainline churches in North America have not realized that the old "just war" theories are outmoded by the new technology of mass destruction. We considered Saddam's call to the Almighty a kind of desecration, but on the other hand, the West's claim to righteousness was a hollow claim. I believe that what this war has shown us is that we need a strong, united religious leadership to help people understand the moral issues surrounding modern warfare.

Leddy: I checked all the official statements and almost all of them were strongly against the war.

Roche: As I read the situation, there was confusion. There were responses ranging from total rejection to grudging acceptance. There were Catholic bishops — important bishops — who issued statements of support because they said it was the only way to contain aggression. Many bishops remained passive even when the massive bombing of Iraq was taking place. The churches as a whole were confused, and in the Catholic Church in North America there was not a consistent, strong message about the immorality of this war.

De Roo: I have another question about the Third World. I'm concerned about what happened in terms of a further distortion of global relationships, because one superpower effectively imposed its will on the rest of the world. It has forced its economic system on the world through the military-industrial complex. How will that be perceived by the Third World? That's a frightening point to consider, and it calls us to go beyond Christian insights that have been too much identified with the West.

Humanity cannot survive on the basis of one Western nation forming a universal police force, acting out of interests that are perceived by many people in the Third World as primarily economic and not based on any common vision or purpose for humankind. When you think of how readily the preservation of the environment was cast aside during the war, the massive destruction that resulted, the full consequences of which we have yet to understand, it is clear that we lack a set of criteria or a vision that could bring the human race together.

Roche: Let's for a moment consider the role of the United Nations in all this. I have just spent a few days at the U.N. in New York and there is strong resentment toward the U.S. underlying almost all U.N. activities today, for having used the U.N. to justify a U.S. war.

However, though it was weakened by the strong American push to provide legal grounds for war, paradoxically the U.N. may have been strengthened because, as a result of the end of the Cold War, the Security Council was able to work together. It is the continuation of working together on an agenda for peace and peacekeeping, for solving problems in the Middle East, that gives us hope that there may be a strengthened role for the U.N.

Leddy: I agree that there are some grounds for being hopeful about the U.N. but I'd also like to agree with Remi's Third World concerns. I think Islam was treated in a very shoddy way during this war. It was presented as a caricature and that is exceedingly unfortunate.

I also want to note with interest — and it goes back to the question of the morality of the war — that a recent Senate subcommittee on violence in America reported that the U.S. is the most violent nation on earth — with respect to rapes, murders, muggings, that kind of thing. I think there's a direct relationship between this and what we have been talking about. We cannot have national political leaders acting on the premise that if you want something you go for it, that might makes right, that the way you get what you want is to use force, without there being a spillover effect on national life. If those principles are acted out on the national level, they will be reflected in the domestic morality. Over and over again, we see that the seeds we are sowing in our foreign policy take root within us, in the heart of our society. These policies are profoundly demoralizing.

De Roo: We are seeing it here in Canada in the violence reflected on television. Even in our relatively quiet neighborhood in Victoria, there is an increasing number of cases of violence related to drugs, to the abuse of other people's property, abuse of other persons. It's a frightening phenomenon and I agree with Mary Jo that there is a direct link between what we allow our public leaders to do and glorify and what individuals will do.

Leddy: We can't glorify the "turkey shoot" on the road out of Kuwait City and then be shocked when some guy walks into McDonald's and pulls out a gun. It's inevitable.

Roche: At the beginning of this war I had a sense of despair, until I remembered the words of Barbara Ward. She often said, with reference to the political stupidities of the world, "I do not have the luxury of despair." None of us can be deterred from getting on with building the conditions for peace. In retrospect, we see that the real winner in this war was the military-industrial complex; the real losers were the people of the Third World, who were marginalized more than ever — the Kurdish people are a tragic example of that.

Leddy: We are all losers....

Roche: Yes. And in this tragic moment of history, as we reflect that only a year ago, when the Cold War ended, we thought we were ready to turn things around, I think we simply *have* to commit ourselves to using the knowledge we have gained over the past several years, positive and negative, to build a new order on the lines of an equitable and sustainable future. As its basis it must have an ethical and spiritual reality. It will demand some radical changes, a deepened awareness of the sacred source of all life and an understanding of the integral relationship of the human species with the whole earth community. We will need to search for a new global ethic for humanity.

De Roo: A beautiful theory, but I think we have to bring all this back home, because I sense at the local level a kind of smug self-satisfaction about the Gulf War, about how efficiently we cleaned up *that* particular problem. The challenge now is to wake up and realize that we have all been deluded

— as Mary Jo said — about the quick solution of problems through the use of force. We are just now beginning to sense the problems of rebuilding after the devastation and trying to restore trust among the nations. In that respect we are in a worse situation than we have ever been in. At our immediate local level we have to revive the peace coalitions which have been badly fragmented because of the war. We have to rebuild those coalitions across denominational lines. We face a real pastoral challenge in our own local congregations in promoting together a spirituality of peace and non-violence.

✠ VIII ✠

THE MANY WAYS
TO GOD

De Roo: Returning from Vatican II, I was all enthused by the gains we had achieved in ecumenism. I won't elaborate on that now. But not long ago I was being driven through downtown Vancouver in the early morning when people were going to work, and I suddenly realized that the phenomenon of immigration had exploded my vision of ecumenism. I became aware, graphically, of what I had perceived mentally for quite some time here on the west coast. As I looked at the people lined up waiting for buses, I saw that the bus stops had become human kaleidoscopes. Every type or colour of humanity was represented. Bus stops reveal the future of the city. The challenge of Matthew 28 to preach the Gospel to all nations suddenly came home to me with an impact it had never had before.

A new question echoed like a refrain through my mind. Are we moving from *what* the Church is to *why* the Church is? Is it time to be less concerned with the institutional framework of the Church, although that is certainly not without its own importance? Time to re-examine and rethink the whole question of the Church's mission? The mission of Christ is meant for all nations. The mission of the Church is to all peoples. Not only are all the nations in a sense "with us" right here in Canada, but increasingly we can see that Christianity remains a minority movement among the nations of the world. This is something we have to think about.

Roche: I too want to begin with a story. When I came to Edmonton in 1965 as editor of the *Western Catholic Register*, a paper founded in the spirit of Vatican II, I found myself frequently invited to Anglican and Protestant churches. Ron Sheppard, now the Anglican bishop in Victoria, was then rector of All Saints' Anglican Cathedral in Edmonton and invited me to speak in their Lenten series. At the end of the series he presented me with a gift, an autographed picture of Dr. Michael Ramsey, who was then Archbishop of Canterbury. I was very touched by this expression of fellowship and friendship.

Indeed, in those years I found myself being invited to speak in far more Anglican and Protestant churches than Catholic churches, and I must say that the welcome I got was in many way overwhelming. It deeply affected me to be received so warmly by those very people that the pre-conciliar Church told me I couldn't have anything to do with. You know, in my boyhood, you virtually had to get permission to go to a neighbor's funeral in a Protestant church! Fortunately, we've moved beyond that.

And I connect my experience with all those churches, with its Christian dimension and openness, with my professional experience in New York, where I would look at the sea of faces, mostly non-white, on the floor of the General

Assembly of the United Nations. Here was another experience of the human kaleidoscope.

I come now to what has been, for me, the most painful
post-conciliar experience. And that is to see, in the last quarter-century, a withering away of the spirit of hope, the movement for unity that was so central to Vatican II. I don't mean
to suggest that no progress has been made in dialogue and
relations between churches, for indeed there has been some.
But Vatican II got it into my head that there was only one
love, only one supper, only one baptism. There was only one
Christ. And yet here were all these divisions. Then one day
during the time of the Vatican Council, when I was on a journey to the Holy Land, I spent a morning all by myself in the
Garden of Gethsemane. Can you picture that? Well, it was
there that the ridiculous division of Christianity hit me full in
the face.

I visited the Church of the Holy Sepulcher, over which
no fewer than six branches of Christianity are fighting to get
control. Jesus must be up there just weeping at the stupidity
that has been endured in the name of Christianity.

Leddy: I hadn't thought to begin with a story, but as both of
you were speaking, a story came to me that might illustrate
the situation we are experiencing right now. It was during the
papal visit to Canada in 1984. When the Pope visited
Edmonton there was to be a great interfaith service, and I was
doing commentary for the papal visit live on CBC-TV. The
service started and there in the sanctuary were Muslims, Jews,
Anglicans, Protestants and so on. The service had been
worked on for a whole year in the Archdiocese of Edmonton,
which is known for its ecumenical, grass-roots theological
dialogue. And the Pope spoke on the light of Christ and how
this was *the* light in the world, the only light. He spoke on the
way of salvation and redemption as if he were preaching in

the Catholic Church. And there it was on the monitors in the
broadcast booth.

I was there with Ted Scott, who was Primate of the Anglican Church, and Peter Mansbridge, who now reads the news
for CBC on *The National*, and we just couldn't believe what
was happening. It was Christian imperialism, and blatantly so.
We scrambled to figure out what to do and the upshot of it
was that, with a quiet chuckle, Ted Scott lobbed me this
gentle little line: "This doesn't seem to represent the view of
the Church since Vatican II." You know, he didn't push it as
far as he could have. It was one of the worst moments of my
life. I didn't want to say that Christ wasn't the light of the
world or that the Pope was dead wrong. And yet the one document of Vatican II that I know by heart is *Nostra Aetate*, and
I really had to say, without blowing the whole thing out of the
water, what the teaching of Vatican II was on the questions of
non-Christian religions and other Christian churches. The
whole incident was shocking because such an effort had been
made to include all the Christian and non-Christian denominations in that papal visit.

Well, I think many of our own non-Catholic friends are
genuinely confused at the mixed signals coming out of the
Vatican. At times there are marvelous statements — marvelous. The recent statement on racism is truly the strongest
statement that has ever been made on anti-Semitism. Yet at
the same time we have the Auschwitz Carmelite monastery
situation, in which many Church persons seemed unaware of
how a cross raised over Auschwitz was an offense to Jewish
memory, and the Pope's meeting with Kurt Waldheim despite
the claims that he was a loyal Nazi during the war.

There is this constant uncertainty as to where we are, so I
myself have wondered about the future of ecumenical and
interfaith work in the Church. But I still find myself extraordinarily hopeful when I think of the Vatican II documents. They

were certainly less than some had hoped, but at the same time, when you think of the long history that preceded them, it was such a momentous, almost miraculous thing that happened in Vatican II. And when I look at how these statements came about — and you know more about this than I do, Remi — it wasn't just out of the blue. The bishops at Vatican II simply ratified a direction that had been set since the early 1900s by various theologians and movements — Anglicans like William Temple and so on. And that long history is my reason to hope that what has been set in motion is really irreversible, no matter how inconsistent the response of some bishops and some Vatican officials. It has taken root in marvelous ways at the parish level, in social action, in theological education. The theological dialogue has been really extraordinary.

De Roo: I don't want to downplay the mixed signals or the blunders in strategy, or the possible lack of judgment of scriptwriters or even local officials in staging that particular talk in that context. However, so as not to get ourselves into too much of a negative mindset, I would like to point out the tidal change that took place at Vatican II. I want to indicate what a couple of the key texts say. What a number of observers considered one of the most important statements of the Council is in Article 8 of the Decree on Ecumenism, *Unitatis Redintegratio*, where it states that the true Church *subsists* in the Roman Catholic Church. That was a reversal of what Pius XII had declared, that the Roman Catholic Church alone is the true Church.

And then there was Article 2, on the hierarchy of truths, which I think is an extremely important operative principle for the future at every level, and perhaps particularly in the understanding of ecumenism in the interfaith sense of the word. It reminds us that while all truths are important, they are not of equal centrality or significance in relation to the core mystery of Christ as the Word of God become flesh. This opens up space for discussion with other Christian bodies. Tie that in with the call to common witness and the fact that, by accepting the other churches as sisters in the Christian household, we are no longer talking about foreigners or even distant cousins, but brothers and sisters. Sisters and brothers within the same family.

I bring these two texts forward as foundation stones on which we can continue to build. And to me maybe the most important element of all is what has happened in these twenty-five years in terms of social justice. I'll take a concrete example. When I arrived here some thirty years ago, I would have been hard put to find a group of people prepared to commit themselves to a common struggle on issues of social justice. And yet I was told the other day that six hundred and fifty people on Vancouver Island can be identified as working together on social justice across all boundaries of race, religion and creed. To me that's a sign that the Spirit is really moving.

Roche: Two aspects of your comment give us a solid reason for hope. There are the extensive official documents moving the Church forward. And in this particular diocese where loving attention has been given to all aspects of ecumenism — and particularly to the social justice sphere — significant numbers of people have been involved in an ecumenical way. But there is perhaps a quandary that we face here, despite the strength of the "Decree on Ecumenism" and the fact that a number of individuals are moving ahead.

For me there has to be a great deal more than this. That indeed was the promise of Vatican II. The hopeful signs in some quarters notwithstanding, the reality is that, a quarter of a century after Vatican II, the movement toward unity has gone so slowly as to justify the use of the words I used earlier:

in many respects it's withering away. Mary Jo mentioned the
question of Jewish relations. I don't see how we can make any
real progress in Jewish relations, or in any interfaith relations,
if we cannot get the Christian ecumenical end moving. In
that respect, the twenty-fifth anniversary of the "Decree on
Ecumenism" went by virtually unnoticed. In my diocese a
seminar was held but the attendance was minimal, and even
then the polarization that exists within the Catholic Church
was all too sadly evident. We had a gathering of about
twenty-five to thirty people, and the first two or three women
who spoke revealed themselves as extreme right-wing
Catholics and attacked the new liturgy as a sort of bastardized
version of Catholic worship in the pre-conciliar age. They
attacked the whole feminist movement for denigrating the
priesthood, they attacked the weakness of the Church's position on abortion and said the bishops were going soft. You
know that line of argumentation; I'm only recounting it here
to indicate the kinds of things a bishop has to put up with.
Here was a bishop present at a gathering, trying to move
ahead. But of course he also has to be concerned about unity
in the diocese.

Leddy: One of the things your example points up very well —
which has been documented by several studies of the Church
in Canada and the U.S. — is that in the past twenty-five years
there has emerged within all the churches this split between
liberals and conservatives, and that people often identify
more with similar people across denominational lines than
with people within their own church who are at the opposite
end of the pole. I can see this very clearly with social justice
activists in different denominations, who find more support
with one another than they do with, say, the evangelical or
fundamentalist group in their own church. It's very interesting: people are grouping across the old boundaries, around

certain interests. In the United States you see this very clearly; you have ultraconservative Catholics like Pat Buchanan and Michael Novak in a common cause with right-wing funda- mentalists like Jerry Falwell. There's a kind of grouping that crosses denominational lines for political purposes. Sometimes this can be extraordinarily positive. I've seen some retreat cen- ters in the United States that truly cross denominational lines, where there is a common interest in a very nurturing sense — and where there is also genuine respect for the differences of each tradition.

De Roo: That focuses once again on a question I raised earlier — a question about mission, and the shift from the concern with *what* the Church is to *why* the Church is. I think we will find that these people are united across denominational and structural boundaries in their vision of what constitutes the mission of Christ, and in their personal and communal com- mitment to work out that mission. This common vision is really showing up in areas like justice and peace, which I see as the most effective contemporary expressions of the Gospel. I think it invites us to identify ecumenism and ecumenical progress less and less with structures. I think we were a little bit naive coming out of Vatican II, thinking that ecumenism would manifest itself rapidly in the coming together of struc- tures. Today we're beginning to question the very wisdom of trying to achieve organizational or structural unity.

That brings the focus back to something else you've heard me harping on before. If I am primarily concerned with the institutional model of Church, then I will hear echoing these objections that Doug has so eloquently placed before us. These people Doug referred to are very worried. They think the Church is disintegrating because they no longer see that clear black-and-white institutional model standing there as the dominant thing. You could even stretch that model a bit to include the sacramental dimension: the institutional/sacramental configuration is very visible. And connected with that model of the Church are those absolute verities, those truths clearly and authoritatively proclaimed on specific issues, providing definitive answers to people in search of security.

Roche: I can well understand that a lot of bishops would be justifiably concerned about the Church flying apart within their own Catholic jurisdictions. And consequently, many of them would be cautious about movements for change. But there is something going on in this conversation that I want to get at, and it has to do with differences in approach. Mary Jo, I must appear to you as something of a contradiction, because I opened our dialogue with considerable emphasis on the Church as the People of God. I cited this as the first thing coming out of Vatican II because it affects everything else. I'm not going back on that.

And yet, at the same time, you've heard me arguing strongly for structural reform. Well, there are two aspects of the Church, the People of God and the institutional structures. I don't think it's good enough to say that individual Catholics, along with other people, can free-float across denominational boundaries to get personal satisfaction. It isn't good enough because what we are left with is a resistance to change by the institutional structures which are the embodiment of the Church in the community, and by people in powerful leadership positions.

I'm saying this isn't good enough, given the promise of Vatican II. What we have in all the commissions and conversations — Catholic/Orthodox, Catholic/Anglican, Anglican/United — are attempts to find some visible sign of the unity of the Church of Christ. Vatican II charted a course in the direction of visible unity. And I'm afraid that the resistance we are now seeing is a result of the misuse of authority within the Catholic Church in this last quarter-century. Instead of the promise of Vatican II, we have a reaffirmation that our Church is indeed an authoritarian-style Church, and this has rekindled some old fears among the Orthodox, the Anglicans and the Protestants. Thus the ecumenical movement is impeded by the persistent authoritarianism within the Catholic Church. For me, that is a structural problem that must be addressed.

Leddy: I want to respond to both of you, but let me start by agreeing with Remi that there has probably been too much emphasis on institutional ecumenism. I think a lot of people just don't want a bigger bureaucracy, for very good reasons. Unfortunately, there are also elements within the Catholic Church for whom institutional ecumenism has become a case of turf war.

But I find that in some of the early Protestant efforts, like the unsuccessful Anglican/United Church of Canada discussions on unity earlier in this century, the barrier was not really theological or institutional. What I learned from history is that churches are not just institutions; in certain respects they are cultures, and you can't just whomp those cultures together. They're like an ethos, a way of being.

Churches have fundamental symbols and traditions, and I don't think we want those differences to go away. So the ecumenical challenge is really to affirm these differences. The theologians told us there was no real theological impediment to Christian ecumenism; several commissions have stated that. There are institutional impediments but, over and above that, there is this delicate question of respecting the variety of almost tribal-like cultures.

De Roo: What you have said is very interesting and very important. I want to pick up on the question of culture and broaden it to the point where I began this discussion. Here we are, back at the core of the new Vatican insights.

Article 44 of the "Decree on Ecumenism" says that adaptation is the law of evangelization. It addresses the question of how the Gospel will reach different cultures. Now, every culture produces its own institutions. And a global culture is evolving which will involve local cultures in very complex ways. So the challenge of evangelization is getting to be a real jigsaw puzzle. What is required is a reconsideration of the very nature of Christology, because Christ is to be proclaimed to every culture and in every culture. John Paul II made this point here in Canada with particular reference to native peoples. Christ becomes human in the culture and through the culture, and native via the native culture. So let me repeat, we are driven to ask the deep question of *why* the Church is. I'm not saying this to diminish the importance of the present institutional expression of the Church. But if we are going to remain true to the Gospel, we will have to become more diverse, more complex. We will require new ways to be Church while maintaining continuity with the past, integrity of doctrine and so forth. We have to allow diversity in order to proclaim the Gospel in languages comprehensible to different cultures.

Leddy: The puzzling thing to me is this. On the one hand, the Church has been able to adapt to a variety of historical situations: the period of Constantine, the feudal period, Renaissance urbanization. There have been a lot of different institutional forms in its history. But on the other hand, we seem to think that what we have now is somehow divinely ordained and that the Gospel is inherently linked to this particular institutional form. Now, I am not willing to say that contemporary Western democracy is somehow ordained by God. I think it's a limited human expression. But I do think a

challenge today is to see how the Church and Gospel message can be embodied in some of these democratic forms.

De Roo: So we're back to one of the central refrains of Vatican
II: expressing the Gospel in different cultural forms. There
has been a relating of the Gospel to Third World development. Now we are moving beyond that model to the model
of humanization. We are saying, not just any kind of "development" but that kind which allows the truly human to
emerge. Notice how many books are being written now
about the humanity of Christ and the relationship of Christ
to culture. First of all we had the idea of converting the
"natives" to make Christians out of them. Now we understand that it's more a question of liberating — liberating persons and cultures from powers that are oppressive and
destructive. And now we are not only recognizing the dehu-
manizing features of poverty and making a preferential
option for the poor, but discovering a reverse evangelization.

The Third World is coming to liberate us! And the poor
are bringing us the Good News based on their fresh experience of the Gospel — something which can crack open a lot
of our stereotypes and a lot of our own cultural assumptions.
This was certainly my experience in Latin America.

Roche: I'm having a great deal of difficulty in this discussion.
I feel for the first time that we are on different planes or in
different places. Maybe that's all right — I don't know. It's
certainly creating tension in me. I have expressed a real pain
in the failure of the post-conciliar Church to live up to the
promise of ecumenism, the promise that we would all be one
in Christ and that there would be a visible manifestation of
this. And I hear both of you saying that you don't really care
about this pain. Frankly, I don't feel the question I have
raised is being addressed, and I think it has to be addressed

before we get to the interfaith question and the multicultural question.

I'm angry that the hope that was engendered in me by John XXIII's openness and embrace of humanity has been repressed in the interval, and that we in the Catholic Church have climbed back into our shell and practice our religion from the viewpoint of the person in the pew, in a strictly denominational manner, with occasional lip service to an interfaith event. We don't even bother any more with the week of prayer for Christian unity — that's how bad the situation is.

Moreover, I'm trying to say that you are not hearing me — that the blockage to ecumenical advance comes from within the set of problems we have addressed in this dialogue. Let me put it this way: if we have an ecumenical coming together of Christian churches, of which the Catholic Church is one, what will happen to the question of how bishops are chosen in the Catholic Church? What will happen to the question of papal authority? What will happen to the question of women in the Church? What will happen to the question of mandatory celibacy? What will happen to the question of birth control? These deep and controversial questions impede our own struggle for development and impede our relationship with the other Christian churches. This is a very serious matter.

Leddy: I don't understand why you say we aren't hearing you, Doug; I thought we *were* addressing your question, though perhaps not in the way you want it answered. First of all, I think I heard Remi and me saying (and we have differences on this, different nuances of meaning) that there has to be an institutional change, that institutions are historical, that they can change and they must change. I was speaking of the need to really democratize the Church. To me, that's the fundamental thing. All the problems you mentioned are just reflections of this need to hear and discern different voices, the voices of different people.

The other thing is that I think some would dispute your sense of where to start. I don't think we have to go step by step. I don't think we first have to get our house in order, then come together with other Christian bodies, then come together with non-Christian religions and finally get on with changing the world. Some would say, for example, that in Christian/Jewish dialogue we can come closer together with other Christians. Or that, to the extent that we engage in authentic dialogue with other religions, we can get off the ecumenical plateau and get things moving. I think that at this point we are on a plateau. You know this is all for the sake of the world. You know we aren't talking about having tea and crumpets and dialogues as pleasant occasions.

De Roo: I want to go back and respond directly to your personal comments, Doug. The pain you are expressing is very real. And it's felt by a lot of people. And I don't profess to have the answers to these issues. In a time of transition, many of the familiar horizons are wavering and many of the structures with which we have become comfortable are crumbling. It's perfectly understandable and very human that we are distressed, in different ways and for different reasons. I often feel very helpless in trying to respond, in trying to reconcile different points of view that sometimes cannot be reconciled. People turn to me that because, as a bishop, I am supposed to represent authority and knowledge in the Church; this in itself reflects a model of the Church that we are now questioning. People desperately want me to assure them that they are right and others are wrong. And I try to say to them, really, from your own chosen perspectives, you are both right. I believe that. We can't all together at the same time have the same perception of reality and the same understanding of what is happening ecumenically.

Having said all that, I rejoice at the fact that there are people like you, Doug, who are angry enough to speak so lucidly and forcefully. Because that is the very stuff that healthy dialogue is made of. We can honestly recognize our limited vision and at the same time express our ardent convictions. Remain in communion with one another, keep talking to one another, and not demand that the condition of dialogue be that other people compromise and come around to our perspective. If all of us pursue the truth with passion and integrity, we will all come closer to the reality and the full truth in Christ.

Leddy: I think what you are saying is very eloquent, Doug, and I think I see where some of our differences are now. I'm not asking you to do anything — I'm not. I'm telling you both what I think and feel, but I'm not waiting around for you to do what I'm doing. I'm going ahead with what I can do and I'm not waiting for the Pope to initiate it. I work with Catholics and Christians from many backgrounds and with people who have no connection with the Christian tradition. All this is entirely in the spirit of ecumenism. I am glad of what you are doing and saying and I approve of it, but I'm not waiting around for structures to change.

Roche: Thank you both for your response to the deep frustration I feel, which I know you share. I too am "going ahead" — that's nicely put. You recall that I spoke about the Roche brand of spirituality and the energy I felt within me as a result of the Council, the energy to move into the political and social dimensions of global security. So I *am* going ahead. And I have relationships with many people, very close relationships, irrespective of the formalities of religion. That's how I'm living my life. To repeat: for the eighteen years I was in public life, I didn't have much time to think about all these questions, but in this new phase of my life I'm struck again by the promise we had in Vatican II. An unfulfilled promise.

De Roo: I welcome the affirmation from both of you that you are "going ahead." You are "doing your own thing."

Leddy: No, it's not my own thing! It's much larger than that.

De Roo: Not in the sense of independence, but you are doing what you think you are called to do.

Roche: That's the way I would interpret it.

De Roo: In a responsible and mature way. And in my heart, as a bishop, I can only rejoice because I see Vatican II alive in you both. I don't think that, even if I had made the most valiant attempts, I could have found two people quite like you to engage in this kind of dialogue before Vatican II. And I'm not waiting to clear my statements or to check that the initiatives I'm taking are acceptable to whatever authority. I'm moving ahead, doing what I feel I need to do.

To the credit of the Canadian hierarchy, not one of my brother bishops has ever tried to stop me or told me to cool it. But I realize that some things I have said and done, other bishops have not been comfortable with. A number of them have said they respect what I am doing. Some even graciously said they admired what I was doing, making clear that they personally wouldn't feel comfortable doing it. And I guess that's healthy pluralism, because it reflects respect for the integrity of other people. Perhaps I am impatient. Anyway, I've only one life to live and I can't sit around waiting. I only hope that increasing numbers of people will feel freer to exercise their own ministries and reveal their own gifts and charisms, without worrying about whether or not they fit into established frameworks.

Leddy: Remi, let me pick up on something you said which strikes me as central to all that we have been saying. You said you couldn't have had this dialogue before Vatican II — but you *could* have. There were lots of people dialoguing before Vatican II. Without that, Vatican II wouldn't have happened. It's very important that we recognize that Vatican II did not just happen in the sixties, and it was not the creation of the bishops. Because if it had been, then it could just as easily be snuffed out by Vatican officials or bishops. In fact, it was a movement — I've said this before — that began around the turn of the century, among women, men, all sorts of different groups. I have just been reading the story of Freiburg, Switzerland, in the twenties and thirties, where a whole trade union was in dialogue with the bishops around the question of "the Church and the World." It was that sort of thing that made Vatican II happen. They were part of the "People of God." That is really what we have to believe, because then we know that this kind of thing cannot just be snuffed out by some edict. Do you understand what I mean?

De Roo: I hear what you are saying, and I accept your thesis that Vatican II didn't just suddenly happen.

Leddy: Didn't just drop out of heaven!

De Roo: It was prepared by movements of which I was a part. Like the lay apostolate movement, I guess. What I was saying was not that we couldn't have had a dialogue — I was having dialogues with all kinds of people before Vatican II — but that our dialogues were not based on the substance we are discussing here. Because Vatican II gave us new insights we didn't have before. It freed me up, as a bishop, to discuss and look at aspects of the apostolate that would never have crossed my mind. I was secretary, before Vatican II, to an outstanding Church leader who to me represented the best model of a truly Catholic bishop. Archbishop Maurice Baudoux, of St. Boniface, was president of the Canadian Conference of Bishops at the opening of the Council, and was largely instrumental in the creative role that the Canadian bishops played. Without the strength and leadership of a man like him, we Canadians would probably have hung back more. In fact, one of the reasons some of us were so involved at the Council was that he plunged right in and carried us with him in his enthusiasm as president.

But my point is that the experiences I had at Vatican II make my perception of reality, my understanding of our church and other churches, my ability to relate to people like yourselves at this level of discourse, completely different.

Leddy: I accept that at Vatican II a lot of insights came to you. And I accept that Vatican II was the event that multiplied those insights and strengthened them. But other people had those insights before Vatican II.

De Roo: In partial form.

Leddy: Well no, in full. If you read Karl Rahner's doctoral thesis, it's all there. If you read Jacques Maritain's books, it's all there — that larger understanding of humanness. That larger understanding of the Church. What they didn't have was a broad base of support.

De Roo: Yes, granted that those seeds of the Spirit were there, but they were not widely accepted. It took the Council to bring them to the level of universal consciousness. Let me give you an example. Certainly some leading theologians had thought about collegiality before Vatican II. But I remember Congar telling the Canadian bishops that the concept of collegiality, the word "collegiality," around which a whole school of thought jelled, was almost unknown before the year 1937. And previous to Vatican II and its acceptance by the bishops, it was not really a term of acceptable discourse. So that's a key example.

Roche: Before we finish on ecumenism, I'd like to raise the subject of intercommunion, which I think is an important question for a lot of people and very germane to this discussion.

Leddy: I don't know — I don't think intercommunion is that big an issue. I don't mind discussing it — I'm just saying that there aren't a lot of people who go to other people's churches.

Roche: I disagree — I think this does affect a lot of people. It doesn't affect me personally because when I go to another church, which I do from time to time, I receive communion without hesitation. And similarly, when I'm accompanied by friends in a Catholic church, I unhesitatingly indicate that if they wish to come to the rail they are most welcome.

Such actions — my receiving communion in a church which is not Catholic or inviting a non-Catholic to receive in a Catholic church — are contrary to the rulings, which hold that communion is the seal of a unity which has already been accomplished, rather than a means to create the unity. I hold the latter position.

Now, the reason I bring this up is because the Eucharist as an expression of Church and an expression of unity was a central theme at Vatican II. I think we do a disservice to the fullness of the ecumenical dimension defined in conciliar terms by holding rigidly to a ruling that bans intercommunion.

As I've said, for me this is not a problem — I don't pay any attention to this law. But that's not a healthy sign. It puts me in the camp of those who follow selective rulings and teachings: if you agree with a ruling, you follow it, and if you don't agree with it, you don't follow it. For a lot of conscientious people, this is a difficult situation. So I'm concerned that there ought to be more active progress on the fostering and promotion of communion as a way to create the unity which seems to be otherwise blocked.

De Roo: What I hear you saying, Doug, illustrates a practical application of one of the most fundamental questions we have discussed, the hierarchy of truths. You do not feel that you are attacking fundamental Catholicity in what you are doing and saying. You are making a distinction between what you think is central, and what is not. This is a very sound principle. One need not be upset by a diversity of opinion in a sphere that is not absolutely core doctrine. There can be greater diversity in Church discipline, a greater variety even in the expression of teachings. Before Vatican II, I don't think many lay people would have been able to make those distinctions and feel comfortable with them. But let me move on to another question which I think we must acknowledge.

One of the weaknesses of Vatican II was that in its decree on relations with Jewish people, *Nostra Aetate*, Article 4, where it had an opportunity to *condemn* antiSemitism, it compromised with a softer word, "deplore." I think, in that instance, the Council was hesitant to face the implications of its own deepest insights. Maybe there were too many political things happening at that time, different crises which had to be taken into account. But we should have made it clear that we recognized our common roots in the covenant, the one

irrevocable divine covenant that we too readily divide into
two separate covenants. Furthermore, we should have recognized our own complicity in not acknowledging our Jewish
sisters and brothers as People of God together with us. We
were arrogantly claiming that title only for ourselves. We
should have admitted publicly our indebtedness to the Jewish
people, and acknowledged our guilt and complicity in crimes
against them which were, in fact, crimes against all humanity.

Roche: I agree. It's one thing to have affirmed in *Nostra Aetate*
that there is a special relation between Christians and Jews.
And we should also note that Pope John Paul II, in visiting
the synagogue in Rome in 1986, did call Judaism "our elder
brother" and spoke of the Jews as irrevocably the beloved of
God. Those are important statements. That said, it must be
acknowledged that the hesitancy and the uncertainty of the
Church are still evident at two important points. First, the
Holocaust — the Holocaust does not occupy the place it
should in the minds of Catholics. I can understand that a
Jewish friend might not feel the long period of anti-Semitism
has been erased by a conciliar statement, or even by Pope
John Paul's statement in the synagogue. The slaughter of six
million Jews, brothers and sisters in the Covenant, is such an
overwhelming fact of history that it ought to penetrate the
depths of our thinking.

The second point where our reconciliation is incomplete is
in the Vatican's withholding of recognition of the State of Israel.
Here the conventions of diplomacy are greater obstacles than
any lack of spiritual connection with the Jewish people. Still, I
wish there were a stronger sense of urgency in the Holy See
about advancing the process of Catholic-Jewish reconciliation.

Leddy: Well, when we consider what has happened in the past
twenty years against the long background of anti-Semitism,

what occurred at Vatican II was a momentous achievement. But for me the Jewish people are the best example of why we really need to remain humble about even this achievement. We are talking about people with a two-thousand-year-old wound. It's not going to be healed that easily. And to the extent that it *has* been healed, it can easily be opened up again. We have to be very conscious of this. As I said earlier, my study of the Holocaust opened my eyes to a lot of things. I agree with Doug that its meaning has to penetrate deeply into our thinking.

There is another point I want to make before we finish this discussion of ecumenical concerns, and I wonder if I could turn to it now.

Last fall I went to a meeting with the Dalai Lama when he was speaking at an interfaith service. It was very, very impressive. There were lots of people there. Convocation Hall at the University of Toronto was filled to overflowing and there were all kinds of political leaders and Church leaders there. The Dalai Lama spoke about peace. People were very moved and I, personally, felt addressed and challenged. This was a man from an Eastern religion but, Doug, he was doing exactly what you have been calling for. He was speaking with a powerful ethical voice. He was listened to. He speaks in a truly universal way, a way people can hear, and he is credible. And he comes with nothing. He hasn't issued any encyclicals. He has no power of money, of institution, of numbers. In a way, he is defenseless. But he is really a man of peace and a religious man. In speaking of conflict and peace, what he asked of us came pretty close to what Jesus would probably want us to do. So a truly ecumenical spirit leaves us open to hear important things not only from other Christians and Jews but from people whose religious traditions are very different from ours.

De Roo: Like Gandhi.

Leddy: Yes, leaders, but also people who are not in positions of power.

Roche: Like Mother Teresa.

De Roo: Well, I'm thinking now of people of the East. People who are not Catholic. Recognizing the presence of the Spirit in other religions is something Vatican II was pretty cautious about. However, this is the direction in which we have to move. We must recognize the presence of God in other cultures. Acknowledge that our understandings of the Church, of the presence of the Spirit, need to be stretched, to be broadened. Even our understanding of Jesus Christ. Who is Christ to these people? Maybe our image of Christ has been so conditioned by our Western culture that we are not able to present the Christ of God to these peoples. It's time to open ourselves to other peoples, other traditions, other cultures.

✦ IX ✦

THE CHURCH AS
COUNTER-CULTURE?

*L*eddy: We have been talking about theological shifts at
Vatican II and, since then, institutional changes —
liturgical changes and so on. But I think for many
Catholics the most immediate change was in certain practices
and disciplines of the Church. For example, we used to eat
fish on Friday, we used to fast before going to communion. I
think many of those disciplines and practices were abandoned
at the time of Vatican II simply because they were seen to be
part of a world-denying or self-denying attitude that we no
longer wanted to support.

My own feeling is that we need to recover a sense of the
importance of practices and disciplines — not in order to
deny the world but for the sake of the world. Because I think
we live in a culture that really mitigates against the possibility
of living the Gospel, and there is an urgency that we be able
to live out — not just talk about — an alternative set of
values. That we not live out of self-interest but live, day by

day, out of a sense that sharing is important. And this can't just be an insight. It needs to be a habit of being. Not just what we affirm at Eucharist but a practice in our daily life. The dominant values of this culture are those of consumerism, and Reginald Bibby has convincingly shown that the values of Church people are the same as the dominant values of the culture. And that to me is the most serious issue we face.

How can we live an alternative set of values? It isn't just a question of theology or institutional change, it's a question of converting life and practice and action. The values of our culture are plastic, replaceable, changeable, disposable. Many of these values are presented through television, which embodies what I see as the predicament of the modern world: we have produced these instruments, these tools, these products, and now they are producing us in turn. We have become, in the inner structure of our being, channel flippers. We go from thing to thing to thing — sometimes, if we have the right kind of flipping machine, we can have two or three channels going at the same time.

I think many people have begun to live a kind of episodic life — they see episode by episode but they no longer see any storyline. And it seems to me that this is very destructive. We have been talking about the story of the Gospel — especially you, Remi. But with the episodic reality of television, many people don't even feel the need for a storyline or a plot. This has wreaked havoc on the ethical imperative of making choices, or making commitments. My sense is that it's not that people are choosing evil. Most people are just floating, drifting, without the intense desire and passion to choose the good. I think Milan Kundera's book title *The Unbearable Lightness of Being* really sums it up. People lack weight in their lives. They lack the habits and practices that would anchor their lives.

The most effective people in social justice and peace are those who lead a disciplined life — and I don't mean by that anything morbid or repressed. They have certain habits of being so that justice isn't just what they do sometimes, isn't just what they talk about, but is a whole way of being. It's not just something on Sunday, or at their local social justice meeting. And at moments I have great hope that this is beginning to happen more generally. Just at an ordinary level, I see the blue boxes going out to the curb every week — people are getting into the habit of recycling. I see another example in our own community: we always set an extra place at the table, so that at every meal we are conscious that we are willing to welcome someone else, other people of the world. It's like the Jewish tradition of setting a place for Elijah.

This kind of practice gets down into the deep structures of your being and becomes an attitude of life. I was very conscious when my dad was dying — and he was really in agony at times — that the only thing that really gave him peace was when we said the rosary, which has that very powerful prayer, "Pray for us now and at the hour of our death." And I thought two things. Yes, Mary was with him at the hour of his death. But I also realized that the prayer he'd said all his life had gone way below any conscious level, and that when you're not conscious any more, that's the level you pray out of. And I felt that quite challenging because it's the same way visions of the kingdom of justice and peace are grounded. Those can't just be conscious efforts. They have to have entered into the deep subconscious of our life to be truly operative and loving.

Roche: I'm very impressed with what you say, Mary Jo, but I see things from a different perspective. I can offer a brief analysis of today's world as I understand it and I can speak about how I *feel* in the world today. I propose to do a bit of both.

Let me begin by talking about the television remote control I'm holding in my hand. This is a symbol of our culture for me, a symbol of the modern world.

As I said when we were discussing prophecy, the modern world has strong positive and strong negative characteristics. On the positive side, the achievements of technology and science have produced a world in which, for the first time in history, we can feed every human being. There is no shortage of food. Through technology there is the medical extension of life, transplanting virtually any organ of life through medical science. There is the new bonding of people through electronic communication and air travel. We have almost immediate access to every part of the world. A huge catalogue of information about how our planet works has been provided by a series of United Nations conferences over the last twenty years.

The negative side: we have used technology to produce arms that can obliterate life on the entire planet. Extensions of the militarism that have plagued the human family from its earliest moments of history are still rooted deeply in the psyche of nations, the psyche of political leaders.

There is frightful poverty in our world — forty thousand children under the age of five die every day. In a week, the number of children who die as a result of water-borne diseases and malnutrition exceeds the number of people who died in the Hiroshima and Nagasaki blasts combined. That was a signal moment of history, but here and now we have this silent killer at work week by week.

There will be another billion people in the 1990s; 95 percent of them will be born into lands that are already severely discriminated against by the world economic system. And the increases of poverty and misery and marginalization have never occurred at so rapid a pace.

That's the world, and it's a great paradox. As a news junkie, one who is a communicator by profession, I almost hate to pick up the newspapers because I realize they will dwell on the confrontations and the negatives. And yet my experience in traveling through the world has revealed to me that there is an immense amount of creativity in progress, and there are thousands and thousands of people who are giving their lives in all manner of creative efforts to improve the human condition.

I come now to my own feelings. In this world I feel marvelously alive. I feel I am sharing in God's process of continued development of the planet. I offer that not as a grandiose claim, believe me. But I do feel blessed — I have to put that right on the table. I feel blessed by health. I have sufficient funds to keep myself alive. I have the blessings of a strong family. I have faith — which gives me a base on which I can stand as I get up in the morning. And I realize that I have an obligation to those around me.

I don't mean to suggest that my life is without pain. My daughter, my severely mentally retarded daughter, is a source of sorrow. (Though I have to add that she is also a marvelous source of strength and joy.) There are strains in my family; there is suffering in the world. I have had my share of frustrations in politics and diplomacy, in dealing with bureaucracies. I too am a mix of the ups and downs of this world. In the final analysis, it is my faith that motivates me, that secures me and enables me to reach out. That's why I am so grateful to the Second Vatican Council — because of what it did to reinforce that faith. So I do not feel myself overwhelmed by the downside of culture.

I come back now to this remote-control device which lets me control the television. Notice the way I put that: I control the television. I don't feel enslaved by it. I don't feel that being a channel flipper is necessarily a bad thing. This device enables me to sustain and affirm my liberation in a culture that is surrounded by all kinds of values I don't share. I can select from thirty or forty channels and I have access to the world. And believe me, that will get even better when we have instant translation of the news from places like Beijing every night. So I have answered the question about how I relate to the culture around me. I can celebrate its achievements and struggle against its destructiveness.

De Roo: Mary Jo, as I listened to you, there was a movement in me that I also experienced in the course of my morning prayer. There I was, alternating between what is known as the Russian pilgrim mantra, "Lord Jesus Christ have mercy on me," and the theme of "Thank you, God, for life, for the resurrection and the joy that penetrates the whole of reality." I don't want to move around like a zombie, like somebody who is already dead. I don't want to feel that the productiveness in me, the energy, the vitality, is not going to make any difference in the world. And as I listened to you, Doug, and heard the very sharp contrast in your own experience between the good and the evil in the world, I caught myself coming back to the same refrain. On the one hand — thank you, God, for all this beauty, for this magnificent planet. And on the other: apologizing to my fellow human beings and to God for the terrible things we are doing to the beauty of creation. And out of all this, I want to share three reflections.

First of all, I would like to say a word about my own self-knowledge — which I hope is a form of wisdom. Secondly, I want to speak of my work. What am I here for? What's my ministry? And thirdly, I want to ask, "Can I make a difference? Can I change anything?" I'll just talk to the first point now and then welcome your response.

When I reflect on the book of the Apocalypse or read about mythic monsters and demons, I say to myself, such language speaks to us today, relates to our own experience. We confront demons in our lives and in the world. This sort of thing is made clear in a contemporary form in human growth programs which raise questions like: what are the sources out of which I operate? What are the fundamental drives that move me for good or for evil?

I know that I need to discover the demons within me. That's why, on retreats and quiet days, I ask myself, what are my personal addictions? What are my dependency syndromes? Unless I raise these to the level of my consciousness and come to grips with them, they will control me. So the first thing I have to do is achieve honesty, self-love, wisdom. Unless I know myself, I can't share the reality of who I am with anybody else, let alone pretend that I have anything to offer to others. It's an illusion to think I can operate out of a position of superiority. We all need the redemptive power of grace. I want to know the presence of that grace within me, the presence of Christ in me, so that my passing through this earth, my walking on this planet, makes a difference.

Leddy: I'm not quite sure how to respond to this. Certainly it's helpful to learn that the two of you, because of what you do and what you believe, don't feel dominated by the culture. But I still think we have to confront Reginald Bibby's statistics, which show that Catholics, Christians in this country, have the same values as everybody else. We've been talking about whether they have traditional values, conservative values, liberal values, Vatican II values, or pre-Vatican II values, and what Bibby is saying is that they have the same values as everybody else. Self-interest is the most important thing. Success is the measure of the person. Look out for yourself. People are measured by what they own, by their positions, by their power, by how they look. Those are the operative values, unlike the stated values that we dispute within the Church.

Let me give examples from within the justice and peace movements, where in the name of the Gospel, in the name of justice and peace and alternate values, we are engaging in something that is deeply Christian and counter to the culture. We want to know we're succeeding in these stated concerns. But underneath these concerns, we are still driven by the cultural norm of success. We won't know we're achieving success unless we "get the numbers," and we measure our success by the number of people at a demonstration, or the amount of press coverage we receive. So there can be a subtle process of manipulation to show that we're winning. There is this competition that exists between different groups. Sheer, raw domination. This happens.

Roche: That triggers something in me. I found it amusing when you said that you are measured by what you do, that your position defines you. When I left the government, I entered a period of my life when I didn't have a job. And nobody was very clear about what I did. But the fact is that I'm actually busier than I've ever been, fighting for minutes to fulfill the commitments I've made in a range of activities. And still people say, "Gee, how do you like retired life?" You know, I'm ready to sock them when they say that. So I take your point: that's how things are seen. The Wall Street banker must be important because he has a big job. But the unemployed single mother who's trying to scrape by is not important because she doesn't have any real status and therefore she has no political clout. She won't be written up in the *Globe and Mail* social column.

But, Mary Jo, is self-interest really a characteristic of *our* times? And raw domination of one by another? Wasn't Jesus talking about this two thousand years ago?

Leddy: I don't think you're really facing the question. Of course self-interest has always been with us, but I'm saying something more than that. I'm saying that the evidence is clear: Christians are simply acting out of the ethos of our time. Here I am talking about the Church since Vatican II: the competition, the power struggle between liberals and conservatives. If each is simply seeking to "win," how different is that from any other power struggle in our highly competitive culture?

Roche: Are you saying that, despite Vatican II, Catholics today are no different from the people around us?

Leddy: An image just came to me that might be helpful. We have been talking about a Vatican II image of the Church as the People of God. Let's say that the operative pre-Vatican II image was the Church as a fortress that defended us against an evil world. I think what the statistics are telling us is that the operative image today is the Church as McDonald's. You go in for a hamburger, for a little sustenance when you feel a need for it, and that's it.

De Roo: I welcome that exchange because I think it relates very effectively to my second point! You've described the operative values in our society — the McDonald's syndrome, the Bibby statistics, the consumer-world syndrome. But the story of God becoming flesh among us, Jesus living our life and showing us a new way, really does make a difference. Now, that comes right home to me, to my ministry, my task as a bishop. It's becoming clear in my own mind, out of my own limited pastoral experience, what that task is. It is to be with people who *are* seeking a new way, who *do* want to change things and not just to affirm the world as it is. Some of these people are the poor, the powerless, the marginalized. There are others who are no longer mesmerized by fantasies of power or prestige or popularity and seek something more transcendent. People who want to get beneath the surface of things, the façades, the masks. People who want to relate the story of their lives to a story that has a greater meaning. Well, the human story has been transformed because God has chosen to become a part of it. This opens up quite new values, presents a profoundly new alternative way of relating to our world and each other.

Leddy: Remi, what I hear you talking about is bringing the good news to a very materialistic society. But I think the Church has so long defined itself as being against Communism, against historical materialism, that it has blinded us to the extent to which materialism is true of us too. We are a deeply materialistic society and I think we have overlooked that, because we say, well, the thing about our society is that we are free and democratic. But I don't see that we are, especially in the United States.

I think democracy in the U.S. is a myth. They had a recent congressional election in which only about 20 percent of the people voted. It was one of the lowest voter turnout rates in the world. Major decisions are made by elite groups in secret, quite outside the democratic process. In Russia the oppression has been clear and the materialism has been obvious. But the situation is much more subtle here. I think Václav Havel was right that the deepest lie of a materialistic culture is that there is nothing worth living or dying for, and I think that's why so many of us are attracted by the Church in Latin America. It's clearer there that the Church has a reason to live and a reason to die. The liberation of people is at stake, and people see the struggle for liberation as something worth dying for — and they believe in the Resurrection. And that's a very powerful witness.

When I show the film *Romero*, people are just so moved at the witness of somebody who had a reason to die and a reason to live. What I said to one group of students was, if you don't know what you are willing to die for, you don't know what you are living for. I don't think many people in this culture do. And I see this as a terrific challenge for us as a Church. I remember talking with a human rights worker in El Salvador who said, "If I die, someone else will take my place." I don't think we have that feeling in the North American Church. The institutional fracturing has left people quite isolated from one another. There's a real loss of community. And I don't see how we can undertake authentic, radical evangelization if there isn't a sense that we are part of a community of purpose. That we are in this together and that, if I fall back, someone will come forward.

I think this sense of shared mission is the hope of the Church of the future. And I don't mean on some vast universal scale, but that at least there will be intermediary groupings and communities of purpose. I'm thinking out loud here, but I don't even think it's desirable any more to have a universal Catholic sense of common purpose and unity. Now, the extreme of that is where the liberals have gone, "doing their own thing." But I think there's an intermediate position, and a hope that while I may not be able to find a sense of common purpose in the "universal" Church, I can still find intermediate groupings on the national level or the diocesan level or the local level, where I'm fully committed and share a sense of common purpose.

De Roo: I just want to make sure I heard you right about the universal common purpose. Because it seems to me that there *is* universal common purpose in bringing the humanity of Jesus into the world in such a way as to humanize creation.

Leddy: Yes, I agree with that as something overall, but I mean something a little more...

De Roo: Specific?

Roche: Don't you think that Christ is essentially counter-culture? I'm thinking of your reference to Latin America. When I first went there twenty years ago, I was scandalized by the alignment of much of the Church hierarchy with the governments oppressing the people. But today people like Romero aren't just isolated exceptions. The identification with the struggle for liberation is not only a cleansing thing for the Church; it gets back to Christ as one who was "counter" culture. So I think we've got to stop weighing and measuring the post-conciliar Church in terms of our own culture. We need to be challenging, not conforming to, the culture. That's the first point I want to make.

The second is this. You are saying that the Church as you see it is not animated with the social justice dynamism of Christ. Is it not possible that the reason for this is that the conciliar values have not been practiced by the Church? The main conciliar values of pluralism, People of God, collegiality and social justice have *not* been practiced. What has happened is that we have actually failed our society by accommodating ourselves to it rather than challenging it. We have made Christ part of the value system of our culture rather than its challenger.

Leddy: I really think we are getting to the heart of the matter. The issue for me is that the Church has to become counter-culture. You were horrified that in Latin America the Church made its accommodation with the military and the powers that be. We haven't — at least in the same way — accommodated any military leaders but we have made our accommodation with mainstream culture — in other words, with the way things are. We have made our accommodation with powers that are far more subtle and probably, therefore, far more dominant.

My biggest problem is not with the conservatives. My biggest problem is with the "McDonald's" approach. I do see some conservatives operating out of the cultural values of domination and control but I also see some very sincere conservatives who are worried that the Church has gone flabby. And I see some liberals, Vatican II liberals, who are seeking authentic Christian life, but I see some of them just operating out of supermarket spirituality. So I would like us to move beyond seeing the conservatives as the major problem.

I'm not sure that the problem is that we haven't implemented Vatican II. I mean, the liberals would say it is. In my view, the problem isn't that we haven't fully lived it. Even if the Church were more pluralistic, more tolerant, I feel we would still be facing this more profound problem. Certainly we would be more a Church of integrity if we had more pluralism and more tolerance and more sense that we are the People of God. But I think we're dealing with the fact that we used to live in a fortressed Church that protected us from the world, and now we live in a Church with a permeable membrane. You know, we can go out into the world — we are all affirming that it's very important for us as Church people to go out into the world — but "the world" can also come in. And in very subtle ways. I don't want us to put up another wall; I don't want us to go back into the fortress. But unless we develop disciplines that enable us to resist seduction by those things in our culture that look so enticing but are ultimately destructive, I think we are in deep trouble.

De Roo: I agree. I don't want to set up walls either. And I want to come back to the expression "Christ as counter-culture."

But first, I'd like to pick up on your critique of the liberal versus conservative issue. Labels are always dangerous because they permit us to reduce people to one dimension, set them aside and not hear what they are saying. I think we need to listen to both liberals and conservatives. But I want to extend that critique to the radicals as well, because the radicals are not all that immunized against the values of our culture. If we want to get down to the real meaning of Christ, we have to get at the values that were operative in his life. He didn't just talk about them. He showed what they looked like. The parables were the living Jesus story just as Jesus was parable in action. It was by doing what he did that he caused people to ask the question, "What's different about this man? What does he mean?" He told parables with hooks in them. The parables made people think. And the life he lived had the same effect.

Now, to get back to the earlier point about contrasts and similarities. You made a point about certain deep similarities between Russia and the United States, except you said the contrasts are more obvious in Russia. I heard the same thing from leaders in Africa. I think of my friend Archbishop Hurley, who was also a Vatican Council father. He isn't a darling of the media like Boesak and Tutu, but he has been doing and saying the same things at great personal risk to his life. When Boesak was speaking at the World Council of Churches in Vancouver, he was asked, "Are you afraid to go back?" And he answered, "No," because back there in South Africa it's very clear which side you are on and it's clear where Christ is being crucified. So the issues are much clearer, much more challenging. The spiritual danger of not recognizing the issues is much greater in our society.

I hear the same message from native peoples here in Canada. As the debate heats up and the confrontations deepen, perhaps we will be forced to indicate more clearly where we stand.

Roche: I'm getting a little nervous. There is a paradox here which I don't pretend to understand. I'm the one who introduced Christ and counter-culture and it has gone in some directions I didn't intend. Are we to deny that Christ can be *in* our culture? Are we to deny the Christ of the stadiums, the Christ of space travel? The world is still developing. I don't think we've reached the acme of all that can be. And I sense in both of you a certain resistance to the coming of what technology makes possible.

Leddy: I've seen the future and I'm not impressed!

Roche: Okay — if you want to say that. I've seen the future and I like it!

Leddy: Well, maybe that's a fair response.

Roche: But I'd like the future a lot better if we let Christ get rid of the imperialistic mindset that still predominates in the Vatican. I'm not afraid of the future. But I do agree with you on one very important point: that for many young (and perhaps not so young) people in our society, there is nothing worth living or dying for. I agree with you when you say that if you don't know what you would die for, you don't know what you are living for.

Leddy: Maybe I could add just one thing, Doug. Catholic education is a real battleground. What's going to be taught in the schools? The conservatives think that if we just give young people clear teaching, they'll be okay — they'll have a Catholic identity and they'll be solid and they'll have weight. And the liberals feel that, well, we have to teach them how to live in the world, how to take our culture seriously, and they don't want to lay some rigid thing on them. And neither really gets to the heart of it: what our young people want is a sense of something worth living or dying for.

De Roo: Behind that conservative-liberal dilemma, you see different models of Church. With the conservatives it's the institutional model, stressing clarity of doctrine, authority, solid structures. Teach them the basics, the three academic "R's" plus the fourth R, religion. The liberals say no, let's downplay our differences and just go with the flow. Christ is *there.* And that's reacted to in turn by the conflict model, the radical model, saying, you liberals and conservatives are both in the grip of past perceptions. We face a new world out there, a world of conflict between oppressors and oppressed, that calls for a totally different approach.

Roche: I want to go back to what Mary Jo said. I'm struck by your words "Catholic education is a battleground." I guess that's right. I've never been able to figure out those people who are against sex education in schools. The same people are against peace education in schools. *They* are the ones who are afraid of the future. They don't understand the sweep of religion through history, in which the deepest values of religion are protected when the current problems of society are addressed on an ongoing basis. Anyway, I see a lot of parents who are disenchanted because Catholic education has been too ghettoized. They want their children to have a wider type of education, particularly in high school and certainly at the university level. And then there are those Catholics who resent the closing of Catholic schools, particularly in the United States, as part of the transition the inner-city parishes and schools are going through. And so a characteristic of our times is that there are a lot of Catholic parents who want Catholic schools to do the job of inculcating a definitive Catholic value system into their children — and they are offset by a number, I don't know the proportions, who are disenchanted with Catholic education because they think that its approach is too narrow and that it insufficiently prepares their children for the waiting world. I don't have any solution to this except to say that the education of young people has got to be sensitive and responsive to the changing world and Church, and not try to protect young people from these changes.

Leddy: I have quite strong feelings on this question. I don't think we can control the future of the Church. When we try to control it, we turn schools and seminaries into battlegrounds. And I find it appalling that we are trying to use these young people, young students, young priests, young religious, to push our agenda. That's not education. Certainly we can say what we think is true, and we can say what we're not sure of. We can offer that to students and seminarians and so on. But the attempts to control, I think, are just despicable on all sides. It's got to stop. It's terrible.

De Roo: Now you have given me a powerful insight into some of the issues I struggle with in education. I'm glad you opened up the question of schooling, Doug. I agree that this is a good lead into thinking about the future. Because ultimately the question of education is central.

Our conversations have sought to clarify what it means to "die before you die," and how we want to live, and what we think about the future. But let me come back to the schools. Here again I expound a favorite theory. As I hear both of you talking, what echoes in my mind is Avery Dulles' proposals about models of Church and Revelation. This bears directly on the question of education. Our model of education is the model of control which you have eloquently described. The concern is with structure, discipline and externals. This amounts to trying to control the future of the Church by controlling our educational institutions. By controlling these institutions, people hope to control the mission. Mission control for the future. Space age stuff!

Contrasted with that is a different understanding of education. In some ways it's new; in another sense, it's ancient. I'm speaking of education which is not primarily content but rather a total life experience. The way we educate and the way we relate to each other within various social and institutional structures is more important than the subject matter we teach. To me the core question is, can our Catholic schools nourish both students and staff, all those involved in this massive, major investment in education? Can we help all these people, through the experience of Catholic schools, to deepen their Christ relationship? To learn how to relate their Christ relationship to the totality of their present and future life experience?

We are only human inasmuch as we relate. The deeper, more extensive, more complex and rich my relationships, the greater depth I have as a human. I mean human first of all in relationship to myself. Self-discovery is one of the key purposes of education. Then there is relationship to others. The child moves from the restricted milieu of the family into the social milieu of the school. In relationship to the larger society, the student becomes conscious of being a citizen. Beyond the social world lies the world of nature; we learn to relate to nature and respect it partly through the very sciences that help us discover how it works. And ultimately there is our relationship to God.

Thus we have a model of education centered not so much on content as on life experience. Education is ultimately grounded in the relationship to God, who is the womb of all life. I see the whole universe undergoing a constant process of begetting, giving and sharing of life from the womb of God. Not a manipulating, mechanical God, but the Source of all life, of all love, a never-ending and evolving Source. That's the framework within which I understand all education.

Roche: That was good, Remi, but you still haven't told us your third point.

De Roo: Okay, my third point. Vatican II said a lot of things about the Church in the world and how the Church and the world should relate, but it didn't really consider the dynamics of effecting change. How do you bring about change? How can all these beautiful visions and images make any difference? So I come to my third perception of what my life task is all about, and that is to be an agent of change. Not only to *have* these operative values that I've gained from the gift of Christ, but to try to transform them into reality. This is an area where I think the Canadian bishops have made a special contribution in their recent statements, and in their pastoral methodology for social change.

It begins with a diagnosis of the situation people are in — social, economic, political. This, of course, is a method used in Latin America, and in other countries as well. It makes full use of the human sciences. *Gaudium et Spes* emphasized — I think in Article 37 — that we depend on the sciences to help us do this analysis, to develop the social critique. But our unique contribution is to do the social critique not only in light of all the contemporary sciences, but also in light of Gospel values. To bring all this together — social analysis, reflection, prayer, discernment and then act for empowerment. This approach gets us well beyond the notion that "Christ is against culture." It relates theology and the social sciences, it involves reflection and prayer and it sees the Church as an agent of change in the world. This is the Church in dialogue with the world, allowing itself to be challenged by the culture, but at the same time letting the Gospel speak to the culture and renew it from within.

✦ X ✦

THE WAY THROUGH
AND THE WAY BEYOND

De Roo: As we look to the future, let me first refer back to one of our earlier sessions. I have been deeply impressed and inspired by a movement that is rising today to a level of greater consciousness, a renewed prophetic tradition in the Church. I remember how excited a lot of people became when John XXIII spoke about the signs of the times, particularly the signs of hope. Waving aside the prophets of gloom and doom, he proposed to bring some fresh air into this dear Church of ours. We need more open doors and windows. And indeed the Holy Spirit used Pope John to awaken the Church to the need to catch up with what God was doing in society and in the world around us. We had to get out of the siege mentality that accompanied the Reformation. We had to open our arms in love to a world needing to be embraced, sisters and brothers waiting to be recognized as such. That spirit really caught fire in the world. I'm very conscious that, despite all the warts on the face of the Church

indicated a true openness and if there were no toleration of
sexism or patriarchalism, if there were a true linkage with
other churches, if there were no banning of theologians who
were trying to open up frontiers, then I'd have more confidence in the synodal approach.

Leddy: Well, I hope we don't get into some kind of hand-
wringing session. On the one hand, the conservatives are
lamenting the passing of the Church they loved. Lament.
Lament. Lament. And then there are the liberals — and
Doug, you've been representative of this to some extent here
— lamenting the lost opportunities following Vatican II.
Now, I understand all that. I think the laments are real and
there's real reason to lament. But...

Roche: Mary Jo, there's a tension between you and me about
how we respond to institutional problems. My view is that
the institution is a key expression of the reform process. This
is why I place a stronger emphasis than you do on the need
for the ecclesiastical side of the Church to get with it. The
fact is that there is a polarization between the liberal and conservative interpretations of the Church at this moment. It
surfaces in every issue we discuss, and it produces a certain
paralysis. In my view, there is a fear in the hierarchy, even
among those who would like to move forward, that there will
be a fracturing of unity as a result of all this turbulence. And
so they pull back. On the one hand, I see in Pope John Paul II
a leader who has a brilliant understanding of the dangers of
both Communism and capitalism. On the other, I see a Pope
who is resisting the necessary ecumenical forward movement
and resisting human justice issues inside the Church itself.

Leddy: Well, ever since the early seventies there has been
growing conflict between the liberals and conservatives

within the Church. It has become increasingly vicious and, I think, increasingly debilitating. And it's a conflict I've been involved in and at times engulfed by. A lot of stereotypes have developed and I'm afraid I have contributed to them, and for this I am sorry. There is the stereotype of the conservatives as the "defenders of the faith." And there is the stereotype of the liberals as subversives who are out to destroy the Church. Another stereotype: the conservatives are ignorant people, uptight and repressed, while the liberals are truly enlightened. All this would be funny except that it has deadly consequences. In some areas of the world — like Latin America — there are deadly consequences for people who are called subversives in the Church. And when you get close to such people, you see how complicated reality is: there are shadows and light in both camps. Among those I would call conservatives in the hierarchy, there is a very dark desire to control — to wheel and deal with the powerful. And as I see it, in the Church, power is often exercised by people who don't have the ability to exercise it in any other area of life. With some, one has the uneasy feeling that, without sex, power becomes a kind of aphrodisiac. On the other hand, there are enlightened conservatives who are people of great fairness, and they have a profound concern for lost meaning in the Church. They need to be heard because they are saying things of importance.

And then there are liberals who simply like to be in opposition. They like to see themselves in a victimized role. Often they are people who live quite comfortable lives, but they have a need to be doing battle with people in authority. But there are also liberals whose desire to be involved in the world springs from a genuine faith that grace and goodness and humanity are to be found there. And they have a profound conviction that God is to be found there, too. So the reality of this conflict is very mixed, and there can be a locked battle between the shadow sides, or there can be dialogue between what is best in both positions.

What troubles me most about this conflict is that I see it as being so protracted. I see no end in sight. So the question is this: how are we going to conduct ourselves in this polarized situation? We can conduct ourselves in a very vicious fashion — we can say, let's eliminate the opposition. The conservatives can try to eliminate the liberals — get rid of liberal theologians, don't appoint liberal bishops. At the moment, this is a highly organized strategy; it's not just happening by accident. And since the liberals aren't really organized, they are just reactive. So it's a very polarized situation and it's very destructive.

But we don't *have* to act that way. We can acknowledge the polarity but refuse to get into the kind of battle where we seek to destroy each other. We can disagree. We can offer critiques and we can absolutely refuse to get into "final solutions"!

But what really worries me about this kind of debate, where we argue about past glories and future solutions, is that we lose the *now*. The real now is neither the past — as we think it was or as it should have been — nor the future, for which people have such vastly different hopes. To the extent that we lose the now, we lose a ground where there is energy and imagination. Part of the problem is that we have been raised in the modern mindset, which believes tomorrow should be better than today. In other words, we believe in progress so we cannot just let tomorrow be; it has to be better, and if it's not, there is something terribly wrong. I think that, in a subtle way, what we know as hope gets confused with this modern view of reality which sees time, which sees history, as progress.

At this point it seems important to say, as Saint Paul says in the fifth chapter of Second Corinthians, "for anyone who is in Christ there is a new world." That means *now*. We know that this is the moment for us because *now* is always the moment of Christ. And it has been very liberating for me to say that the now is no better and no worse than the past. It is exactly the best place to live and to hope and to be. It's no better and no worse than the future, either. And I think living in the now means being *critical* — as I have already said. It means to critique the cultural reading of reality. It means to be able to see, as Gerard Manley Hopkins says, that "the world is charged with the grandeur of God," and to see that even in the Church. I think I'll just leave it at that, because to me it's so basic. It's not that I don't sense certain trends for the future. For instance, I'm very sure the women's issue is going to get worse in the Church before it gets better. But I have to let go of this focus on the future. The only thing I know of the future that gives me hope for the Church and the world is that there is life to be found in being with the poor, and for the poor, and in a certain sense becoming poor — I mean humble and poor of spirit. I'm not saying that because of any evidence, but I really do think that is what Jesus tells us.

De Roo: I am happy to hear you say there is only the now, because — especially since Vatican II — I believe now is the only time to live. As a result, I am not in the chorus of those who lament. That doesn't mean I'm not aware of lots of problems. But I prefer to give thanks to God for what is now, for what is happening now, what is possible now. It's put very simply and eloquently in verses fourteen and fifteen in the fourth chapter of Ephesians: "Speaking the truth in love, we are to grow up in every way into him who is the head, into Christ, from whom the whole body joined and knit together by every joint with which it is supplied, when each part is working properly, makes bodily growth and upbuilds itself in love." Living the truth in love, doing the truth now.

I want to give a concrete illustration, an application of this in terms of the synodal principle here and now in our diocese. I don't think I came through all that clearly when I was talking earlier about the synodal principle.

Five years ago, after a number of consultations throughout the diocese, we agreed that we were ready for a synod. Not the juridical type of synod seen too frequently in the past, which is primarily a legislative model, but a truly pastoral synod. We did not begin with an agenda: the moment you dictate an agenda, you pretty well precondition the direction in which you are going. We did not prepare expert position papers: no matter how brilliant they may be, they too tend to circumscribe the agenda; most people will not recognize in them the reality of their lived experience. We simply began with the newly recognized principles of adult education and adult faith development. We called the people themselves into synod. First, we invited people to get together to share their stories in groups or circles, at the parish level, in homes, in living rooms, wherever. We asked them to share their stories and to listen to what the Holy Spirit was saying through the experiences of their sisters and brothers. The next phase was to remember the story of the Church, the Story of Jesus and of our tradition, and in the context of that *"remembering,"* to compare their own stories with the broader story of our faith community through the centuries. In the light of all that, they were to propose what needed to be done, here and now, on Vancouver Island, to be faithful to the Spirit and to prepare for the third millennium by shaping a renewed vision of the Church.

There were only two rules laid down. First, there would be no censorship of any kind. Everyone's proposals would be honored. We would keep a master book where all those proposals were recorded. Once made, they became the property of the total faith community of the diocese, and anyone who wanted the information could have access to it, to enrich it with further insights. The second rule was that there would be no arguing, debating, voting, no majority/minority reports, no polarization. We would follow communal spiritual discernment principles, which meant that in prayerful assembly we would listen to one another. We would not move until the entire discerning community was prepared to accept the new direction. The widespread sharing of wisdom brought in a thousand proposals. Granted, they are not an encyclopedia of Catholic doctrine. There are many gaps. But I believe they faithfully reflect the lived experience of the people.

In the next stage, we proceeded to assess all those proposals. We noticed that almost a quarter of them had to do with social justice. To me that was an indication of the concerns of our people. Now, I believe this is very critical, and at the heart of Vatican II: to believe in the authoritative witness of baptized people, confirmed, matured in faith, who have received the Eucharist. Like everybody else in the Church, we are under the obedience of faith as presented by the Scriptures. We must be a listening and learning Church before we claim to teach. I won't claim any miracles. But I am persuaded that our synodal process constitutes the most creative and powerful thing that has happened to our local church since Vatican II. A book telling our synod story is in preparation.*

Roche: The conciliar work of the Church on Vancouver Island is surely something to celebrate. And you have made it very clear that what you have described comes out of the main themes of Vatican II: the equality of all in baptism; the "People of God"; the scriptural and eucharistic framework of the Church; the ecumenical nature of the concern for justice and peace issues. You have picked up the central themes of Vatican II and certainly you are implementing the collegial

* *Forward in the Spirit: Challenge of the People's Synod*, Diocese of Victoria, 1991.

nature of the episcopal leadership. Now, when I offer a critique of the Church, it is not intended to be a lament. We ought to note, however, that what we have on Vancouver Island is singular.

Maybe I am a kind of joyous critic. Is that a contradiction in terms? There are things I celebrate and things that really make me angry. But one thing is clear. I do not see how we can bypass the institution. For this reason, I'm concerned about the credibility of the institution on issues of public policy: on the great themes of social and economic justice as well as world peace, themes which need to be addressed. I understand the slowness of institutional change and in one sense — following your lead, Mary Jo — I would say that the petition in the Lord's prayer which says, "Give us *this* day our daily bread," is what really sustains me. Today is really all I can handle. But it is my experience that for the Church the *now* is being jeopardized by its sluggishness in the face of so many of the urgent questions of the time. I know God didn't promise us a Church all tied up in a nice red ribbon. Ultimately our hope lies in something beyond institutional frailties. But I object when the institutional forms get in the way of people hearing the Gospel and learning just what it was about Vatican II that opened up the Church in such marvelous ways.

Leddy: I hear in what you're saying a very sharp critique of what has happened and is happening in the institutional Church. But I see on the other hand what Remi is saying about the synod in his diocese in Victoria. What he is doing is in fact creating an alternative. Both things are very important for change. One has to name clearly what's wrong. But that's not enough unless there are some very concrete ways in which people are actually creating alternatives. A lot of people will never leave what's known — no matter how uncomfortable and painful it is — unless they see another way available.

I wouldn't be prepared to say that diocesan synods are *the* hope of the future. I think some of them may be, but I think there are many other hopeful alternatives. Think of the new palliative care ministries, for instance; that's one simple example. I really agree with your critiques, Doug, but it seems to me that it's very important to be engaged in constructing new Christian ways of living and serving. And it's very important for my freedom that I not spend all my energies battling with Church officials and thus, in effect, giving them power over me. I don't want my agenda to be the institutional reality of the Church. But if I spend all my time critiquing the institutional Church, then I'm letting it dominate my life. And, really, that goes nowhere.

Roche: I want my agenda to deal with the preservation of God's planet. That demands an end to militarism. It demands an end to extreme forms of poverty and environmental devastation and desecration. That's my agenda, and as a politician I need help from the moral leadership of the world, because these are all essentially moral issues. I'm not getting that help.

Leddy: Maybe you're looking in the wrong places.

Roche: Where should I look?

De Roo: Maybe I should refer now to the question that some people have raised about the possibility of an eventual third Vatican Council.

Leddy: I certainly haven't raised it.

De Roo: No, but the question has been seriously proposed. I want to say that, in my view, such a Council would not be the place to look for answers to the questions Doug is raising. And I want to explain why I think this way. Let me give my reasons.

First of all, at Vatican II we recognized other faith communities as sister and brother communities. So we could not now address the kind of questions Doug has raised except in that broader context. Secondly, many other Christian churches relate to one another and work with one another through an existing ecumenical association, the World Council of Churches. We could not act without full consultation with that body. Thirdly, at Vatican II we moved not just in an ecumenical direction but also in an interfaith direction. No event has given that movement more visibility than the meeting not long ago of the leaders of world faiths at Assisi. Pope John Paul initiated that meeting, and I think it marks a new phase in religious history. A further reason is that the Vatican has been too identified with Western society and the Western worldview. Until the Vatican effectively breaks out of that straitjacket, it will not be heard as a fully credible world voice. And finally, the issues we are facing are too vast to be addressed by one religion alone. Indeed, answers will only come from serious dialogue between the leaders of religions and the political leaders of the world. We need to bridge the gap, not only between religion and politics, but between religion, politics and science. These areas have been separated from each other partly through the legacy of the Enlightenment. They must now be drawn together. We need a holistic language of meaning to address the kinds of questions Doug was raising.

Leddy: Where I differ from both of you is that I don't think religion should be identified with religious leaders. For instance, I don't really think it makes a big difference whether the Pope is against nuclear deterrence. My experience is that papal documents are largely unknown except to the Catholic literati. Where people have learned that peace is a Catholic issue is when people like Dorothy Day or the Berrigans or Thomas Merton have taken public positions. Those people have far more impact on the world at large than official Church statements, because they get good media coverage. People know about them and the stands they are taking. And this is an indication that leadership actually comes from the people — from the People of God, if you like. I'm not saying it's either-or. I'm not saying the Pope shouldn't make statements on important issues. I'm just saying that we shouldn't assume that the Church's voice is only heard in official pronouncements, or that the Church only acts at the "official" level. It's very instructive for us to think about the great changes that have recently occurred in Eastern Europe. Those changes didn't occur because the Vatican made a pronouncement or because some official passed a decree. They were truly people's revolutions.

De Roo: But just let me interject that in invoking the synodal principle — following Vatican II — we were calling not only for the witness of the head but also for the witness of the heart and of the body. This, I think, is complementary to what you have said. I'm in agreement with you. Leadership and witness come from all parts of the world as well as the Church.

Roche: This discussion is still revolving around my question, "Where should I look for moral leadership on the great questions facing humanity?" I realize that the four great movements of this century — for political liberation, for civil rights, for environmental protection and for women's rights — all developed because people concerned about those questions came together and stirred up still greater concern, until politicians were forced to pay attention. But as a politician I have found that public opinion is ill informed, is weak on other very major questions — like poverty and peace. It's partly because of the ambiguity in, for instance, the question of nuclear deterrence. And the media doesn't do all that good a job — in its short, thirty-second clips — of interpreting and clarifying difficult moral issues. So where do I look? I have often looked to the Church to provide ethical discernment and I haven't found it — with some notable exceptions.

De Roo: Doug, would you accept as a fifth great movement the awakening to historical consciousness of the native peoples of the world? I think this is a momentous development of our time, and it has certainly come from the aboriginal peoples themselves.

Roche: Yes, I definitely would, although I guess I had subsumed that development under movements of political liberation.

Leddy: Doug, I really think you are caught in a contradiction. Either you say that leadership comes from all sorts of people among the "People of God," all sorts of different people at different times, or you deny your own very emphatic point about the importance of the People of God and say that the only place to which one looks for leadership is the hierarchy. And I venture to suggest that more people have learned about the Catholic understanding of peace from reading Thomas Merton than from reading papal encyclicals.

Roche: But think of the impact of the Canadian bishops' statement "Ethical Reflections on the Economy." That's the sort of thing I'm calling for.

Leddy: But "Ethical Reflections" got criticism because it was so particular. It didn't just articulate principles. And there was a whole debate over the appropriate level on which episcopal statements should be made. "Ethical Reflections on the Economy" dealt with very specific questions. I happened to like it — I thought it was great. But I'm not sure you would like it if the bishops got specific on certain other questions — like sex, birth control and so on. Catholics don't want that. This is the problem.

De Roo: A clarification: "Ethical Reflections" did not come only from the bishops. It was drafted by the Social Affairs Commission, of which I happened to be president at that time. It resulted from consultations with all sorts of knowledgeable people, so there was input on specific issues from people competent to speak on those questions, a point the media picked up at the time. So that document got considerable attention because it had sound social and scientific substance. It contained theological and ethical judgments but these were set within a very careful social analysis. It certainly didn't just deal in generalities.

Leddy: Well, my point is that the reason it cut some ice was because it was so specific. Often such statements are so vague as to be meaningless. And because it was specific, it was controversial. It angered some people. But I think we have to be prepared to pay a price when we make a statement. It can cost something if one takes a stand that runs against the grain of accepted prejudice!

Roche: I've been expressing my critique of the institution but I don't think I've really indicated the ground on which I feel hopeful. My hope is that, in this great transformative moment in history, this time of conflict at very deep levels, what the Church has given me through its teaching, through its sacramental and communal life, may be experienced by others. I don't expect that the vision of the Church I found at Vatican II will be achieved in my lifetime, so I take comfort from the words of Reinhold Niebuhr that nothing worth achieving can be achieved in our lifetime. But if you want to talk about Vatican III, I'm ready to start working for it!

De Roo: Well, I've already expressed my cautions about Vatican III. When I look ahead, I think of three things I learned at Vatican II that I need constantly to keep in mind.

First, through Vatican II I came to see myself as a bishop being a servant of the people in this diocese. All the people in this diocese are called to ministries of equal dignity and in many different capacities. In the practical urgencies of day-to-day life, it's very easy to lose sight of this, to slip back into older episcopal patterns. Like all Christians, bishops are called to be servants.

The second thing I learned was that to be more fully and authentically a Catholic was to open myself up to the wisdom and experience of sister churches and other faiths. Indeed, what I learned from Vatican II was to respect the totality of human experience and to be open to new ways of understanding reality. This I see to be the way of the Spirit, and in its own particular way it was the ministry of John XXIII that made it possible for Catholics to appreciate this.

The third point — and it has been very much reinforced during our time together this week — was that the study of the Scriptures, dialogue with each other, the pastoral ministry, the sacraments, are all part of the celebration of Christian life. The heart of Christian life *is* celebration. It's a process of enrichment and celebration. And I guess, Mary Jo, that this is very much a matter of the here and now. It is this here-and-now reality that will sustain us in the future.

About the Authors

Mary Jo Leddy, a Sister of Scion, was a founding editor of *Catholic New Times*. She is a broadcaster, writer and social activist who protests on behalf of the world's dispossessed. A native of Saskatchewan, she now lives in Toronto.

Bishop Remi De Roo, a bishop in Victoria, B.C. for three decades, experienced Vatican II. An author of several books, he argues that "Christians are obliged to change the world."

Douglas Roche, former Member of Parliament and Canadian Ambassador for Disarmament, was founding editor of the *Western Catholic Reporter*. A writer and lecturer, he lives in Edmonton, Alberta.